A2 Drama and Theatre Studies: The Essential Introduction for Edexcel

A2 Drama and Theatre Studies: The Essential Introduction for Edexcel builds on the skills developed during the AS year to provide clear and informative guidance to Units 3 and 4 of the specification. The textbook provides further information on rehearsing, performing, directing and textual analysis, together with new material on deconstructing a script, devising theatre and preparing for the final examination. Features of the text include:

- overviews of specification and assessment requirements;
- written and practical exercises;
- a glossary of useful words and terms;
- in-depth analysis of the three key plays – *Dr Faustus*, *Lysistrata* and *Woyzeck*;
- extension exercises to stretch the more able student;
- worked examples to illustrate best practice;
- sources for further study;
- advice on study after A level.

Written by a senior examiner and a principal moderator, this book and its companion volume for AS level offer informed and supportive exercises to ensure that students reach their maximum potential in achieving A level success.

Alan Perks is a senior examiner. He works regularly with students and teachers across the key stages on individual projects and long-term drama strategies. He also teaches across the age ranges, including the A level course, part-time in a school in Derbyshire.

Jacqueline Porteous is a Principal Moderator with over 20 years of teaching experience in the discipline. She teaches the A level course and leads a Performing Arts Faculty.

A2 Drama and Theatre Studies: The Essential Introduction for Edexcel

ALAN PERKS AND JACQUELINE PORTEOUS

LONDON AND NEW YORK

First published 2010
by Routledge
2 Park Square, Milton Park, Abingdon, Oxon OX14 4RN

Simultaneously published in the USA and Canada
by Routledge
270 Madison Avenue, New York, NY 10016

Routledge is an imprint of the Taylor & Francis Group, an informa business

Typeset in Charter by Keystroke, Tettenhall, Wolverhampton

Printed and bound in Great Britain by MPG Books Group, UK

British Library Cataloguing in Publication Data
A catalogue record for this book is available from the British Library

Library of Congress Cataloging in Publication Data
Perks, Alan, 1956–
A2 drama and theatre studies : the essential introduction for Edexcel / by Alan Perks and Jacqueline Porteous.
p. cm.
Includes index.
ISBN 978–0–415–43658–8 (hb : alk. paper) – ISBN 978–0–415–43659–5 (pb : alk. paper) 1. Theater. 2. Theater–Production and direction. 3. Drama. I. Porteous, Jacqueline, 1961– II. Edexcel (Organization) III. Title.
PN2037.P44 2009
792.071–dc22 2008013906

ISBN10: 0–415–43660–5 (hbk)
ISBN10: 0–415–43661–3 (pbk)
ISBN10: 0–203–87119–7 (ebk)

ISBN13: 978–0–415–43660–1 (hbk)
ISBN13: 978–0–415–43661–8 (pbk)
ISBN13: 978–0–203–86701–3 (ebk)

Contents

List of illustrations vii
Acknowledgements viii

PART I: GETTING STARTED WITH THE A2 YEAR **1**

1 Introduction 3
2 Making good use of this textbook 6
3 Theatrical timeline 15
4 Two golden rules 18
5 Who are they? Examiners and moderators unmasked 20
6 A final few words before you get started 22

PART II: OVERVIEW OF UNIT 3 **23**

7 Research and exploration 27
8 Development and structure 38
9 Performance 47
10 Evaluation 52
11 The Supporting Written Evidence Document (SWED) 58

PART III: OVERVIEW OF UNIT 4 **63**

12 The demands of section A 84
13 The demands of section B 100
14 Exploring interpretations for section B 111
15 The texts for section A and section B 116
16 The role of director in section A and section B 120
17 Annotating the text 128
18 The demands of section C 131
19 The historical periods 146

20 Theatre evaluation 152
21 Deconstructing the questions 158

Conclusion: drawing the course together 160
Appendix 1: drama school or drama degree? 163
Appendix 2: useful websites 165
Appendix 3: further reading and suggested viewing 169
Glossary of useful words and phrases 173
Index 178

Illustrations

2.1	The Globe Theatre	14
4.1	Use the word-count facility on your computer	19
II.1	The three possible routes for Unit 3	26
7.1	The library will be able to help you find books and resources	28
7.2	Can you tell the difference between a SWED and a SWEDE?	29
7.3	Keeping a notebook is a key tool for drama research	29
7.4	Medals	31
7.5	Remembrance Poppies at Menin Gate, Ypres, Belgium	32
7.6	A WAAC's call-up papers and travel documents	33
III.1	Claire Higgins in *Hecuba* by Euripides at the Donmar Warehouse in 2009	75
III.2	Zoe Wannamaker in Shakespeare's *Much Ado About Nothing* at the National Theatre in 2008	79
18.1	Joanna Lumley and Annabel Scholey in Anton Chekhov's *The Cherry Orchard* at the Sheffield Crucible in 2007	132

Acknowledgements

The authors would like to thank the Drama Department and Drama students at The Ecclesbourne School, Derbyshire, for all their creativity and hard work, with particular reference to the class of 2008, the class of 2009, Jade Richards and Monty Till.

Thanks also to Edexcel for endorsing the book, and to the many drama teachers and students who have shared their thoughts with us along the way. Thanks to Ruth Williams and her students at Bishop Gore School, Swansea for permission to reproduce extracts from theatre evaluations.

A word of thanks, again, for those who have quietly supported from a distance with a cup of coffee or glass of wine, and to our respective four-legged friends for regularly reminding us when it was time for a walk.

The authors and publishers would also like to thank the following for their kind permissions:

- Chris Webb for the cover image from a production of *Hetty's Dream* by Tony Jones and Tom Elston
- Guardian News & Media Ltd for permission to reproduce 'When Travesty becomes Tragedy', by Duncan Campbell
- Alena Melichar for permission to reproduce the image from *Hecuba*.
- Catherine Ashmore for permission to reproduce images of *Much Ado about Nothing* and *The Cherry Orchard*.

GETTING STARTED WITH THE A2 YEAR

PART I

1 Introduction

It is always good to know where we are coming from at the start of a new academic year, and one of the first things we need to do is to re-establish very quickly what we understand by drama and theatre in relation to this A2 year of the course. As a starting point for the AS year, we felt that this was useful for students just so that we all know what to expect from the A2 year. It could be that it is even more relevant now as we head into the second, and final, pair of units of the course.

In broad terms therefore, drama is mainly concerned with the process of exploring and is about using a range of techniques to access the given material, often in workshop activities, and theatre is about engaging an audience through a range of performance techniques and elements following a period of preparation and rehearsal.

The Edexcel GCE Drama and Theatre Studies Specification states that:

The A2 year requires you to demonstrate knowledge and understanding of:

- At least two more published plays of which one must be pre-twentieth century.
- The connections between theory and practice demonstrated through a range of forms, genres and performance styles.
- The directorial overview required in the interpretation and realisation of a theatrical performance.
- How relevant research supports practical work.

As an A2 student it is expected that you will develop:

- A more advanced level of performance and/or production skills.
- The ability to think independently, make judgements and refine your work in the light of research.
- The ability to analyse the ways in which different performance and production elements are brought together to create theatre.

How do we go about it then, building on the skills that were developed in the AS year? The important thing to remember is that you have chosen to continue with Drama and Theatre Studies and you will have had a good reason for doing so. It may be that your AS year produced results that encouraged you to continue. It may be that it was always your intention to take the course through to the end of the A2 year. Whatever your particular circumstances, it is worth your while having another look around you at the start of this phase of the course. All the other people in the room will have good reasons for being there too – perhaps the same as yours, perhaps not, but think about this:

Once again, you are all in this together.

Those people sitting around you are going to continue to support you in getting the grade you want from this course, building on your achievements in the AS year, and you will be doing the same for them. We stated in the Introduction to the AS book that this course is about you being part of a group, actively engaged in a range of activities. Having completed Units 1 and 2 you will be fully aware of what we meant by this, and the fact that you are still here is an indication of how effectively you were able to contribute to the group's success in the AS year and, for you, how much you were supported by others in exactly the same way. You are much more on your own in the A2 year with Unit 3, making demands on you and your group for which your teacher can only guide you, not tell you what to do. This may sound like something of a relief – we all enjoy independence and being able to make important decisions about our work without being unduly pressured to take the work in a direction we do not want to take it. With this independence comes responsibility, however, for you to ensure that every person in your group is able to access the marks available for this unit.

It has to be said right from the start, and very clearly, that there is absolutely no point in continuing with this course if you are going to find it difficult to work with others, without the close supervision or guidance of your teacher. If you think this is going to be the case, then you need to consider your position within the group very carefully. Your teacher will, of course, have an input and not allow you to go completely off the rails with Unit 3, and will probably have more of a direct input into your preparation for the written examination that is Unit 4, but he or she is not allowed to direct your work for performance in the A2 year.

Should you decide to continue – and we hope you do – then the good news is that the A2 year is more about you and your ideas than the AS year.

You will not have achieved what you have to date working in isolation. This course is about you in relation to others and nobody in the room around you can succeed without you all working together and getting to grips with the demands of the two units that will complete your A level study.

Look at your achievements to date, either in terms of UMS scores or grades – or a combination of both. Whatever points you have accrued cannot be taken away from you; that is your starting point for the A2 year and it is already effectively 'banked' for you to build on in this second half of the course. Everything that you have been part of in the AS year will directly impact on your contributions to the A2 year; nothing should be ignored or forgotten. You will have developed skills that you can now use in taking your experiences as an individual to the required level in order for you to be able to access the higher marks in both of the A2 units. There is no point looking back and resting on your laurels; you have to see the AS year as the starting point that will take you into the demands of the A2 year. It may be a good idea to work with a partner early on in the new academic year and list the skills you think you have now acquired that may be of use when looking into the new year. Keep the list in your notebook or, if this is a class activity, keep it in a flipchart for you to refer back to when you feel as though Unit 3 is stalling and you are struggling for ideas about how you might be able to take it forward.

It is not enough to have done well in the AS year and to expect those points already accumulated to grow by themselves. What you need to do now is to be focused and to keep questioning to find new ways of extending and developing your knowledge of theatre and performance, and your place within that in relation to the full A level.

We hope you will continue to be challenged by the course and by the demands of the A2 year and that you will rise to the challenge, pushing yourself harder in order to achieve more.

Some things about the A2 year will be more straightforward than others, and some activities will engage you more effectively, but, at every stage, you need to be looking to focus on the task, to be clear about what you need to do and to get on with it. You will be largely responsible for Unit 3 with your teacher guiding you but your teacher may lead you more when it comes to looking at the demands of Unit 4. We hope this textbook will help you in the structuring of your work.

2 Making good use of this textbook

There are a few basic facts about the A2 year that you need to be clear about before you go any further. These will help you to access the two units and to make good use of this textbook. In Unit 3, your teacher is also your assessor with responsibility for marking your contribution to the unit against the published criteria. Your teacher will be leading you into the unit with an understanding of what is required in order for you to be able to access the marks, hopefully building on your AS experience in order to help you to focus. Every task set, therefore, leading up to you developing your Unit 3 performance, will be set for a purpose and with the assessment criteria in mind. There is no time for a half-hearted response to anything; you must remain focused at all times and keep an eye on deadlines your teacher may set for you.

You must meet your deadlines – so that your teacher can meet deadlines set by the exam board that are final.

In Unit 3, the deadline for the final submission of work is set each year by the Examination Boards, and, except under exceptional circumstances, there is no variation to this date and no extension. It will probably be the case that you will perform Unit 3 well in advance of the May deadline in order for you to complete your Supporting Written Evidence Document and have the whole unit wrapped up and ready to send off to the Examination Board.

In Unit 4, the date for the Written Examination is fixed each year by the Examination Board. As with all written examinations for all subjects it cannot be changed, so the June deadline is there for you to meet and to work towards.

The A2 year, then, is about these two units, and there is a lot of hard work ahead, but think about the rewards along the way and the skills you are going to develop alongside those people sitting in the room with you. All of you will inevitably affect each other's grades, which is both reassuring and a little unnerving. We hope you will find the A2 year enjoyable as well as rewarding, and that the challenges you will face will equal anything else you will encounter in other areas of the curriculum at this level of study. The top grades are there for the taking in a specification that recognises and rewards the contribution of the individual within the group.

There is no reason at all why you should not be aiming for an A* grade at the end of the course. You need to be realistic, however, when looking at the marks you have already accumulated and you will need to seek clear advice from your teacher as to what is both a challenging and a realistic goal for achievement at the end of the course. Whatever your target grade, you are going to have to work for it – to build on the marks you already have from the AS year – and the work starts here.

Drama and Theatre Studies demands many different things from students, and talent alone is not enough to see you through. We have never yet come across a student who did not tell us they would like a Grade A or an A* at the end of the two-year course. If you are prepared to work at it and want a chance of achieving a higher grade, then the extension material and homework activities will really help you to develop your work. You need to talk with your teacher and ask for a realistic assessment of where you are now and what you need to be achieving in the A2 year if you wish to achieve the higher grades. Higher education preparation will really kick in during the first half of this year and you will need to have an idea of an estimated grade to put on your UCAS application. Your teacher will be realistic with perhaps a touch of aspiration in this grade and it is only an estimated grade; it is not guaranteed nor should it be seen as an absolute. You need to be very clear with your teacher what your chances are of achieving this grade and what you need to do in order to break down some of the potential barriers for your success.

In line with the aims of the Young Gifted and Talented Programme (YG&T), the extension activities included in this textbook offer more advanced tasks to raise standards and to give you access to formal and informal opportunities to help you convert your potential into high achievement. You can find out more about YG&T at http://ygt.dcsf.gov.uk/.

EXTENSION MATERIAL AND HOMEWORK ACTIVITIES

Throughout the textbook, there are shaded boxes to illustrate particular points. Whenever you see one of these boxes, there will be a task that you may wish to follow up. Remember that this is your A2 course. Your teacher will be there to guide you in lesson times, but there is so much more that you can do to develop your studies and, of course, gain a higher grade. There are particular activities you can be engaged in to help you to prepare for the written demands of the A2 year for example. A great deal of what we offer here as extension activities has this focus.

The shaded boxes will usually offer extension material or homework activities and represent an invitation for you to get involved. They are only suggestions; as you work through the book, you may think of other related activities that could help you to increase your subject knowledge, particularly with Higher Education and Drama School potentially in mind. Our intention is to point you in the right direction in a generic way; your response will need to explore in more detail the information we present here.

If you want a higher grade, we strongly recommend that you explore the information in the boxes, preferably for homework or in your free time.

PRACTICAL EXERCISES

Drama is a practical subject, and the best way to understand it is both to see live theatre and to actively participate in it. Practical drama lies at the heart of Units 3 and 4, and there is no better way to prepare for performance or to explore texts in relation to the written examination than to be up on your feet and improvising, rehearsing or trying out ideas to develop your understanding of how to support the production process. As you start the A2 year, you may already have decided that you are a performer for Unit 3, but don't let this stop you trying out a range of other practical activities (e.g. having a go at costume design or directing a scene). Similarly, you may feel that your main interest is in technical theatre, but, likewise, to experience the devising process of Unit 3 from the actor's point of view will enhance your overall understanding of the process and may help in giving you more of a sense of the overall process when it comes to looking at Unit 4. Whatever your starting point, the advice that we offered in the AS textbook is, we believe, still relevant when planning for the A2 year.

Never spend too long discussing whether something will work or not; explore your ideas practically, and the answer will become obvious.

WRITTEN EXERCISES AND THE QUALITY OF WRITTEN COMMUNICATION

The quality of written communication is very important and it is assessed to varying degrees across all of the units of this specification, but particularly in Unit 4, which is the written examination that is worth 30 per cent of your A level marks. If you have been given the opportunity to write regularly throughout the course to date, it will make a real difference to your ability to write well in both your coursework for Unit 3 and the written aspects of the examination. The quality of your written communication has to be taken into account, and this is not simply a case of being able to spell the drama words correctly; it is more than that: it is also about the way you express yourself on the page in the context of the material you are being asked to write. Both of the A2 units have written elements, with Unit 3 having the Supporting Written Evidence for which you are assessed.

There are word limits in place for the Supporting Written Evidence, in the same way as there are time limits for the performance work, further details of which we explore in Chapter 3. You really need to be aware of how important this could be to your eventual marks, so it is a good idea to switch on to this now. By recognising the need to write clearly and concisely and by being able to structure responses to practical drama that are evaluative and analytical, you are setting yourself an approach to written communication that will enable you to access the demands of both A2 units, including the written examination that is Unit 4.

So as to get you into our way of working, we are now going to give you an extension activity to have a look at. This activity is typical of the type of challenge you will find throughout this textbook and it should challenge but not baffle you. This activity is in relation to Unit 3, and ideally it should be attempted in pairs.

Extension Activity

Responding to a given stimulus

In pairs: on an A3 sheet of paper write the word DISPOSSESSED.

Between you, list as many meanings for this word as you can think of in five minutes and then, in another ten minutes, take each of the meanings you have listed and expand with an outline of what you might be able to do with it as a devised drama.

Share your ideas with another pair and then, between the four of you, select the one that you think is the most challenging for possible Unit 3 development and map out in general terms where you might see it going in a preparation time of six to eight weeks. You have 20 minutes for this development.

As a group of four, present your ideas to the class for observations and comments.

For both of the A2 units, you will need a notebook that you can use as a working diary to record activities, your feelings about them and the learning experience you have been involved in. This notebook could be the one you used in the AS year if there is still space in it, making a connection with the past to push you forward into the future. You should be used to writing about what *you* do, what *other* people do, reflecting on your own work and that of others in the class and at the theatre if the notebook has been an essential item in your AS year toolkit. The reflection on the experience is important, developing your critical faculties in ways that will help you to access the higher level of marks for your written communication in both of the A2 units, but particularly in Unit 4. It is not enough at this level of study to 'tell us about'; you need to develop the capacity to 'tell us about and reflect upon', offering critical evaluation of your work and that of others. Part of this process is also about considering what else you could have seen or done; in other words, some alternatives, as there are always other ways of approaching things in the theatre.

Have a look at the sample diary extract that follows. This is one way of presenting the information. You may have a way that you think is more appropriate for your own notes. The extract will give you some idea about the kinds of things you may write down and suggested approaches that may work for you. The important thing is that you see the notebook as a diary, as this will help you to write in the first person and to be more reflective of the process and your contribution to the activity. If you have your notebook from last year, have a look back and see how much information there is in there that you would have forgotten about if you had not written it down.

SAMPLE DIARY EXTRACT, UNIT 3 DEVISING

Stimulus Exploration: *Road* by Jim Cartwright

Date: 7 October 2009

In the lesson today, we looked at two extracts from *Road* by Jim Cartwright. I read Eddie in one of the extracts. We talked about Eddie and Brink as characters and were given some background on the play and about Jim Cartwright.

This was useful. It filled in some of the gaps, looked at language and boundaries, and what was acceptable (some strong stuff!). We talked about whether it was necessary. Did it shock? Possibly then, not so much now but also probably not necessary now. We discussed the 1980s – unemployment, miners' strike, Thatcher.

> We talked about the relationship between Eddie and Brink and what might have happened to them. We set an improvised scene in which we had to imagine either Eddie or Brink now returning to their home town after years away – somewhere – and what their reactions would be. We are looking at the 1980s as a starting point at the moment – lots to think about. Need to look at theatre at the time and music. . . .
>
> I'm Eddie – lots to think about. He's been to prison, I think. . . .

At the start of the course, your teacher will have prompted you into recording information in your notebook, but, by now, you should find that you are doing it automatically – and it is a useful habit to be getting into for other subjects too!

In compiling your diary or notebook for the A2 year, it is never enough to write what you did or what somebody else did. It is really good to get into the routine of giving your opinion about the work and reflecting upon it in a critical way.

Two key words to always bear in mind are:

ANALYSE

and

EVALUATE

analyse
When you write objectively about something, explaining it by breaking it down into sections, supporting your opinion with 'why' and 'how'.

evaluate
When you offer a balanced opinion, looking at something from both sides and justifying your conclusions. Both words mean you are offering an opinion.

You will read more about these two words as you go through this textbook, and hear more about them from your teacher. The decisions you make in relation to Unit 3 need to be supported by reasons, and your reasons are a development of your understanding of the experiences you have had to date as a student of drama. Do not postpone written work; it will be much more difficult to try to remember it later than tackling it straight away. Good-quality writing has a freshness and personal tone to it which tells the examiner or moderator that you have been involved with the activity and have understood it clearly. It should also demonstrate an understanding of the language of drama. Your notebook or diary is a great way of getting yourself into the habit of writing and reflecting as you go along.

THE LANGUAGE OF DRAMA

Drama and Theatre Studies uses specialist phrases and terms. You should always use the language of drama when it is appropriate to do so whether you are speaking or writing. When you reach Unit 4, part of the assessment of your written communication will be based on your use of appropriate drama and theatre terminology. The more familiar you are with words and phrases – and their spelling – the more you will be able to demonstrate your understanding in your written work. The two units of the AS year were really useful for getting to grips with drama words and phrases and exploring them in the context of work heading towards A level standards. There is an emphasis across the specification as a whole in the quality of your written communication which is taken into account in the awarding of marks, so it is a good idea for you to switch on to this right from the word go in the A2 year. Some words and phrases will come more naturally to you than others and will be more familiar to you through usage. For all of us, though, there really should be no excuse for misspelling words such as 'rehearsal', 'improvisation', 'character', particularly as these words are frequently spoken in this course and should almost as frequently be written down. You should also be familiar with the words relating to the texts for Unit 4, and there should be no excuse here, either, for not getting the spelling of names right in relation to the chosen texts. If you are not sure how to spell something, then you must ask. You will probably find that others around you are wishing they had asked too – but are really pleased that you did!

There is no shame in not knowing something; the shame is in not finding out when you realise that you don't.

Another thing that this textbook will do is to highlight and define specialist terms as they arise and, once you have understood their meaning, you should make use of the language. Once you have understood the specialist term or word, the writing of it in context is usually enough to indicate that you have understood it, making it unnecessary to explain what a dramatic term means within the body of your written work. A common mistake is to write something like this: *'at this point in our devising we decided that we needed to explore the work of a particular practitioner in order to help us to come to decisions about the overall style and feel of our piece. We decided to look at the work of Steven Berkoff. Berkoff is one of the leading exponents of physical or total theatre. He was born in . . .'.*

You can always assume that the audience for your written work already knows and understands the who and the what of the practitioner. For Unit 3 it is the why of your decisions and the outcomes that will be of more interest, particularly when you only have a limited number of words with which to play.

There is a glossary at the end of the book that explains a range of terms and builds on the one that is at the end of the AS textbook. While there will inevitably be some overlap, there are words and phrases here that are more appropriate to the A2 year than the AS year.

You could start on your A2 glossary now, in fact.

Extension Activity

The language of drama and theatre

And the meaning is? Using the glossary, find out the meaning of the following words and write a sentence for each in your notebook to demonstrate your understanding.

1. Devising
2. Artaudian
3. Proxemics
4. Tragedy
5. Forum theatre

Have a go!

INCREASE YOUR KNOWLEDGE

Drama and Theatre Studies is such an exciting, vital and expanding world that there is always something new to learn. Your teacher will introduce you to new plays, playwrights, genres, practitioners and much more.

Greek drama began approximately 2,500 years ago, so already there is all that theatre history to explore; and, thinking ahead to Unit 4, some background knowledge of Elizabethan theatre could prove useful. You should be able to gather a lot of information just by looking at Figure 2.1.

The theatrical timeline (Chapter 3) gives you an overview of some of the major theatrical developments and places them in their historical context. It is always useful to know what was going on in the wider world while Shakespeare was writing *Hamlet* or while Harold Pinter's *No Man's Land* was receiving its première.

Figure 2.1
The Globe Theatre

3 Theatrical timeline

A basic knowledge of theatre history will really help you put your work into a broad historical context. The timeline produced on pp. 16–17 gives an overview of the past 2,000-plus years. A number of the major theatrical developments are outlined in the timeline, but, like everything else we offer you in this book, it is not the whole story. There are gaps here for you to fill in, and these will depend a great deal on the texts and practitioners your teacher chose to study with you for Unit 1 and the choices made for performance texts for Unit 2. The time periods for Unit 4 are highlighted in this timeline. Whenever a small 'c' is used, it is an abbreviation for the word 'circa', which means 'around'. In other words, the date is approximate. It is around the time specified.

Extension Activity

Theatrical timeline

Create your own theatrical timeline over the past 2,000-plus years using different plays to the ones listed overleaf.

Or

Find other plays written by these well-known playwrights listed in this timeline.

GREEK THEATRE (2,400 YEARS AGO)

480 BC – 406 BC Euripides, *The Trojan Women*, *The Bacchae*
495 BC – 406 BC Sophocles, *The Theban Plays*, *Antigone*
525 BC – 456 BC Aeschylus, *The Oresteia*
456 BC – 386 BC Aristophanes, *Lysistrata*

Lysistrata is one of the possible set texts for Unit 4. Unless your teacher is certain that this play will not be studied for Unit 4, it is best *not* to study it for Unit 1 or use it as a stimulus for Unit 3, as you cannot use the same play for two different units. There is nothing to stop you reading it as part of your background research, of course.

MIDDLE AGES

1564 William Shakespeare born in Stratford upon Avon

Mystery plays
Plays that tell the story of the Christian calendar, dating from around the fifteenth century.

Morality plays
Fifteenth century. Plays that had a strong moral content, that taught the audience something (e.g. *Everyman*).

ELIZABETHAN THEATRE (450 YEARS AGO)

1576 The first Elizabethan playhouse opens
c.1592 Possibly the first performance of a Shakespeare play
c.1580 Christopher Marlowe, *Doctor Faustus*
1612 John Webster, *The White Devil*
1642–1660 Theatres in England closed due to the Civil War
1675 William Wycherley, *The Country Wife*
1706 George Farquhar, *The Recruiting Officer*
1775 Richard Brinsley Sheridan, *The Rivals*

Faustus is one of the possible set texts for Unit 4. Unless your teacher is certain that this play will not be studied for Unit 4, it is best *not* to study it for Unit 1 or use it as a stimulus for Unit 3, as you cannot use the same play for two different units. There is nothing to stop you reading it as part of your background research, of course.

1800 **NINETEENTH-CENTURY THEATRE (150 YEARS AGO)**

1879 Georg Buchner, *Woyzeck*
1879 Henrick Ibsen, *A Doll's House*
1890 Henrick Ibsen, *Hedda Gabler*
1895 Oscar Wilde, *The Importance of Being Earnest*
1896 Anton Chekov, *The Seagull*

Woyeck is one of the possible set texts for Unit 4. Unless your teacher is certain that this play will not be studied for Unit 4, it is best *not* to study it for Unit 1 or use it as a stimulus for Unit 3, as you cannot use the same play for two different Units. There is nothing to stop you reading it as part of your background research, of course.

1900 **TWENTIETH-CENTURY THEATRE (100 YEARS AGO)**

1912 George Bernard Shaw, *Pygmalion*
1923 George Bernard Shaw, *Saint Joan*
1939/40 Bertolt Brecht, *Mother Courage and Her Children*
1945 J. B. Priestley, *An Inspector Calls*
1949 Arthur Miller, *Death of a Salesman*, *A View From The Bridge*, *The Crucible*
1955 Tennessee Williams, *Cat on a Hot Tin Roof*, *The Rose Tattoo*, *The Glass Menagerie*
1956 John Osborne, *Look Back in Anger*, *The Entertainer*
1958 Shelagh Delaney, *A Taste of Honey*
1963 Joan Littlewood, *Oh! What a Lovely War*
1965 Joe Orton, *Loot*
1965 Edward Bond, *Saved*

1966 | Tom Stoppard, *Rosencrantz and Guildenstern are Dead*
1969 | Steven Berkoff, *Metamorphosis*
1973 | Peter Shaffer, *Equus*
1973 | Athol Fugard, *The Island*
1974 | Alan Ayckbourn, *Absent Friends*
1974 | John McGrath, *The Cheviot, the Stag and . . .*
1977 | Mike Leigh, *Abigail's Party*
1982 | Caryl Churchill, *Top Girls*
1986 | Jim Cartwright, *Road*
1992 | Tony Kushner, *Angels in America*
1995 | David Hare, *Skylight*
1997 | Patrick Marber, *Dealer's Choice*
1999 | Richard Norton-Taylor, *The Colour of Justice*

2000 | TWENTY-FIRST-CENTURY THEATRE (MODERN TIMES)

2000 | Sarah Kane, *4:48 Psychosis*
2000 | Joe Penhall, *Blue/Orange*
2003 | Liz Lochhead, *Thebans*
2003 | Martin McDonough, *The Pillowman*
2004 | Alan Bennett, *The History Boys*
2004 | David Eldridge, *Festen*
2006 | Simon Reade, *Private Peaceful*
2007 | David Hare, *The Permanent Way*
2007 | Gregory Burke, *Black Watch*
2007 | Polly Stenham, *That Face*
2007 | Nick Stafford, *War Horse*
2008 | Yasmina Reza, *God of Carnage*
2008 | Tony Harrison, *Fram*
2009 | Samuel Adamson, *Mrs Affleck*

Throughout this textbook, you will see reminders of when you could further your own knowledge of a particular person, event or theatrical element. In order for you to be able to make good use of this textbook, you need to see this as an opportunity to learn something new. You will almost certainly be able to connect any extended learning experience back to your own work.

4 Two golden rules

At this point it is probably worth noting two of the golden rules of A2 Drama and Theatre Studies:

1. DEADLINES ARE DEADLINES ARE DEADLINES

If your teacher gives you a deadline for either written or practical work, it is your job to meet that deadline. It is usually given in good time to allow your teacher to respond to your work before it has to be recorded or submitted to the Exam Board. The May deadline for Unit 3, for example, is for your teacher to submit work to the Exam Board. This means that your teacher will need it well in advance of the deadline in order to assess it before submitting it. Whether there are nine or thirty-nine of you in your group, this process will take time, and your teacher will want to give it his or her full attention in order to make sure you achieve the best possible mark for your efforts. It is very much in your interests to keep up with deadlines.

2. THE WORD LIMITS ON ANY WRITTEN WORK YOU SUBMIT FOR UNIT 3 ARE MAXIMUM LIMITS

The Exam Board has stated that there will be no tolerance here, so there is no point doubling the word count in the hope of doubling your marks. It does not work like that. Anything over the published maximum number of words will be ignored by the teacher-assessor and by the moderator. Similarly, anything over the time limit for the devised performance in Unit 3 will be ignored by your teacher-assessor.

Keeping a word count

The easy way to keep a track of the number of words you have written is to use the word-count facility on your computer. Select the tab marked *tools* and click on the *word count*; this will tell you the number of words you have used so far (see Figure 4.1). A lot of people leave word count activated all the time, as it is really useful for making sure that coursework is of the required length. It is good practice to work to a word limit, as it is probably important for all of your subjects at this level of study.

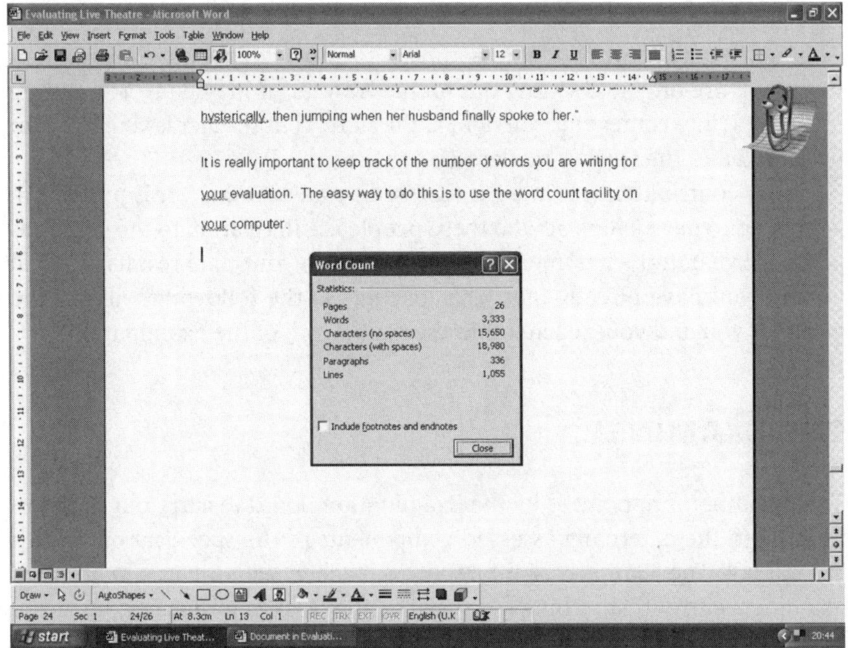

Figure 4.1
Use the word-count facility on your computer

5 Who are they? Examiners and moderators unmasked

Although it may seem a little premature to go into details about examinations when you are only just setting out on the A2 year, it may be worth putting the process into context for you right at the start. Your teacher is your assessor for Unit 3 and the work is moderated.

Your contribution to Unit 4 is assessed by an examiner. It is probably a good idea to have a look at who these people are in relation to the demands of the A2 year and what impact they can have on your final results. We will assume you have already met your teacher, so the following will put the work for you and your teacher into the framework of the examination.

THE EXAMINER

The Examiner is appointed by the Examination Board to carry out duties in relation to the externally assessed components of the specification, in this case Unit 4. The Examiner is or has been a teacher, with the vast majority of examiners currently teaching the specification – ask your teacher: he or she may be an examiner.

Examiners are trained every year to help them to apply the agreed standard to their work in centres, and it is compulsory for examiners to attend a standardisation meeting before they are allowed to mark exam papers. The standardisation meetings are organised by the Examination Board and are led by the Principal Examiner – the person who is responsible for ensuring the standard of marking is maintained from year to year in that unit. It is important for you to realise that each separate question on your examination paper for Unit 4 will almost certainly be marked by a different examiner in the electronic marking system that has been adopted by Edexcel. This could mean that in a group of ten students you would potentially have thirty examiners marking your Unit 4 work, three for each examination booklet. We will go into more detail about the implications of this in Chapter 6 on Unit 4.

THE MODERATOR

The Moderator is appointed by the Examination Board to carry out moderation of the internally assessed components of the specification. In Drama and Theatre Studies this means in the A2 year, Unit 3. The Moderator is or has been a teacher, with the vast majority of moderators currently teaching the specification.

During your contribution to Unit 3, your teacher-assessor will make notes that will eventually help him or her to come to a decision about the marks you will be awarded for your contribution to the process of devising and to the performance itself. At every stage of the process your teacher-assessor is looking for opportunities to reward your work against the published criteria. Your teacher-assessor is not looking to penalise you for anything. At the end of the Unit 3 time period your teacher-assessor will award you marks against the published criteria and submit these alongside a written summary of why you have been awarded these marks. The Moderator's job is then to look at the evidence submitted and decide whether or not the mark you have been given reflects marks for work of a comparable standard across the country. If it does, then your teacher-assessor's mark will stand. If it does not, then the Moderator has the job of adjusting the mark to bring it into line with the national standard. In some circumstances the Moderator may request further evidence of work from your teacher-assessor so it is really important that all of your work is kept safe and secure until the very end of the moderation process.

SUMMARY OF THE PROCESS FOR EXAMINERS AND MODERATORS IN THE A2 YEAR

- An examiner will mark your work in Unit 4.
- A moderator does not mark your work but checks the marking already done by your teacher as assessor.
- Many examiners are also moderators and many teachers are moderators and examiners.
- Examiners and moderators meet on a regular basis – either in person or electronically – in order to ensure that a standard is maintained throughout the examination series, and each specification has a chief examiner who has an overview of all of the individual units and is the ultimate connection between the examining teams and the subject officers or assessment leaders within the examination boards.

Have a look at Edexcel's website at www.edexcel.org.uk. You will probably be surprised at the size of the organisation and the range of qualifications and other services offered.

6 A final few words before you get started

At this point in the AS textbook we talked about the creative process and how drama as an experience relies heavily on your imagination and collective input. Many of you will be making decisions during this year about your future and wondering whether or not to take your love of drama and theatre on to the next level. We cannot advise you on this but what we can say is that for everybody who does set out to pursue a career in theatre there are about another five or six who, in ten years' time, may wish that they had done so. Whatever you set out to do, do not forget that there are endless possibilities for you to demonstrate your skills in the future.

Many careers are open to Drama and Theatre Studies students including management, personnel and social work, team management, and jobs requiring analytical and presentational skills. Popular career destinations include teaching and careers in the theatre or the media. Taking Drama and Theatre Studies will equip you with some important skills for your future career. Two of the qualities most valued by employers in applicants are literacy and creativity. Drama and Theatre Studies will demonstrate that you can work productively as part of a team and that you can demonstrate initiative and imagination in creating new opportunities.

You can be reassured that Edexcel's Drama and Theatre Studies specifications have gained a fantastic reputation over the years with higher education providers, drama schools and potential employers. There is proper anecdotal evidence of this but there is also hard evidence from real people – people just like you – entering university or employment, and effectively using their Drama and Theatre Studies-related skills to develop and enhance future learning.

With an overview of the A2 year in mind, it may seem that it is heavily orientated towards written work. While it is true that Unit 4 is a written examination and your written contribution to Unit 3 is assessed, there will be a balance of activity that your teacher will be able to maintain with you, but, in order to be able to access the wider theatrical world – if that is your intention upon completing this course – you must recognise the structures that need to be in place to help you develop your understanding.

We will now take you through the demands of the two A2 units and give you some ideas for accessing the higher level of marks for each unit.

OVERVIEW OF UNIT 3

PART II

Unit 3 is one of the two units you need to study in order to complete the A2 year, and probably the one that you will begin to work on when you return to the Upper Sixth or Year 13 in September. Essentially, you are going to work in a group and produce a piece of theatre to perform to an invited audience. Unlike Unit 2 where you had to use a script, Unit 3 may be script based, entirely devised (created by your group without a script), or a combination of script and devising.

The Unit is worth 40 per cent of the A2 year and is coursework. The mark allocation will be looked at in greater detail as we go through the requirements of the unit, but you will be assessed on:

- your contribution to the process
- your actual performance
- on a written evidence document that you submit in support of your work.

Your teacher may well be doing some work for Unit 4 with you alongside Unit 3, but Unit 3 will take up about one term of work. As it is worth 40 per cent of the marks for the A2 year, it is logical that it will take up about 40 per cent of the available teaching time.

ASSESSMENT OBJECTIVES FOR UNIT 3

- **AO1**: Demonstrate the application of performance and/or production skills through the realisation of drama and theatre.
- **AO4**: Make critical and evaluative judgements of live theatre.

The assessment criteria are broken down into four distinct areas:

- *Research and Exploration* which carries a maximum of 15 marks.
- *Development and Structure* which carries a maximum of 15 marks.
- *Performance* which carries a maximum of 15 marks.
- *Evaluation* which carries a maximum of 15 marks.

Each of these four assessed areas will be discussed in detail, with reference to both a play and a stimulus in the following sections.

GROUP SIZES

The minimum group size is three and the maximum group size is six. There are pluses and minuses in small groups versus larger groups, but, as you are working more independently in the A2 year, we have found that groups of around four or five students tend to work the best. The minimum performance time is 15 minutes which would be appropriate for a group of three students, and the maximum performance time is 30 minutes which would be aimed at the larger group of, say, five or six students. A good guide is to aim for about five minutes for each group member.

- Three in a group = 15 minutes (minimum).
- Four in a group = 20 minutes.
- Five in a group = 25 minutes.
- Six in a group = 30 minutes.

No group should exceed 30 minutes.

SCRIPT-BASED WORK

If you decide to do script-based work for this unit, your teacher may choose the script for you. However, it is not another Unit 2 group performance; you have to see the script as a stimulus or starting point to create your own version or interpretation of the script. Some people call this 'deconstructing' the script. For example, imagine you have chosen to base your work on *Macbeth* by William Shakespeare and your class is split into two separate groups, with four people in each group. Group one decides to do a version (or interpretation) from the text to show that Macbeth himself is really a good man who makes poor decisions and is driven by his wicked and greedy wife, Lady Macbeth. However, group two decides that Macbeth is a cold-hearted, scheming villain who, along with his wife, is intent on power and destruction. Both groups aim to devise a performance of around 20 minutes' playing time, and both groups choose to use specific lines from the text to reconstruct a version of the play that reflects their chosen interpretation. The lines they choose to re-create their own particular version may be similar or totally different. There may even be small areas of overlap, but, with the use of different costumes, the addition of sound, non-verbal language and directorial decisions, they produce two entirely different 'takes' extracted from the same play.

DEVISED WORK

Many of you will not have been involved in devised work since GCSE, assuming you took GCSE Drama. Devised work usually begins with a given stimulus or focus and is developed through research and improvisation. It is a very time-consuming, creative and often frustrating process, but is extremely rewarding when things go well. Assume for a moment that you are in the same class as the eight students doing the scripted versions of *Macbeth* described above. Your group of four students choose not to base your work on the actual play *Macbeth*, but you take up the themes within the play such as revenge and power, and devise your own 20-minute play based on those issues. You don't even need to look at a script at all for Unit 3. Your teacher could give you a series of workshops on any issue, theme or story, in fact any stimulus of their choice, and from that starting point you can devise a piece of theatre.

SCRIPT AND DEVISED DRAMA

At GCSE this is often referred to as 'the third way'. It means a combination of script and devised work. Sometimes when you are trying to get the best 20 minutes you can from a play that actually runs in performance for two and a half hours, it is difficult to keep the sense of the plot or the structure of the play. In this unit, you could legitimately add words of your own in between lines from the script to make it make sense. Alternatively, you could add devised scenes of your own to provide a modern contrast to the original text. Your piece may be mainly devised, but you choose to add the poignancy of a well-known poem or a quote from a play that gives relevance to your devised piece.

Other factors

There are many other factors to consider as you approach Unit 3, such as the style of your piece, the influence of practitioners, theatre productions you have seen and your intended audience. These factors and other issues will be looked at in more detail as we move on to the nuts and bolts of Unit 3.

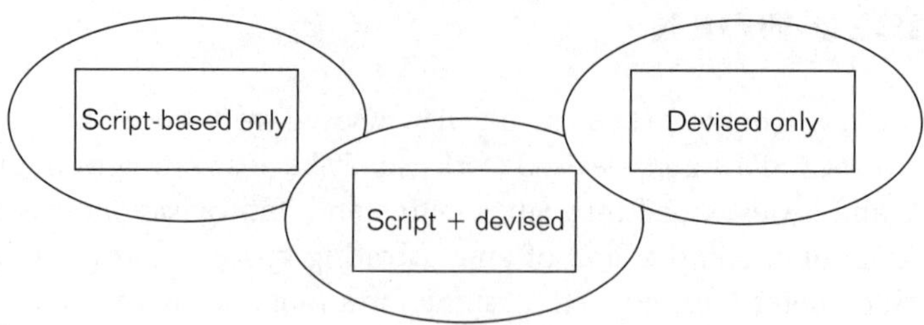

Figure II.1
The three possible routes for Unit 3

Extension Activity

Take a play you know and do the following things with it:

- Imagine you are the director: how would you stage the play if you were to choose a Brechtian style?
- In the style of Artaud?
- Extract only the key themes and issues from the play and use these issues to form the basis of a devised play. Can you plot a scenario using these themes and issues?
- Choose a character from the play. Is it possible to re-create the play told from that one character's point of view?

7 Research and exploration

The focus of this chapter is to show a range of ways that you could research and explore the stimulus that your teacher gives you.

- Unit 3 is marked out of a total of 60 marks which is scaled down to give 40 per cent of the A2 overall, or 20 per cent of the marks for the total A level.
- A quarter of the available marks are given for your research and exploration (i.e. 15 marks out of 60).
- An outstanding level of research and exploration is described in the specification as follows:

  Students demonstrate outstanding depth of research that is far-reaching and comprehensive. It is clear how the research has directly influenced performance outcomes and practice for both self and others.

When you start Unit 3, usually in the autumn term of Year 13, your teacher will give you a stimulus from which to develop your work. It should be substantial in terms of the subject matter it deals with, or the genre it presents, and should be wide open to interpretation, so that your group can take it forward in a range of different ways. Your goal is to create and perform a piece of theatre arising from the stimulus and, in order to do this, you will have to research and explore the stimulus for some considerable time as you embark on the process of creating theatre.

The stimulus could be a range of factors; for example:

- A playscript (as long as you haven't studied that particular play for any other unit)
- A picture
- A photograph
- A story
- A newspaper article
- Some music

- A series of objects (e.g. an old locket, an engraved brooch with the words 'Baby' on, a Death certificate, a police report)
- A fable/legend
- An issue (e.g. assisted suicide, fraud, debt, eating disorders)
- An incident from a different historical time period
- Site-specific work (e.g. you visit a disused factory)
- An audience is specified (e.g. pensioners at the local stroke club)
- A piece of theatre-in-education.

Ideally, whatever the stimulus is, it should fire your imagination so that you can begin on the initial task of researching and exploring ideas that may be developed into a piece of theatre. Your teacher will have the final say in the stimulus and you may not be given a choice.

As we look at the skills involved in researching and exploring in this chapter, we will look separately at two different kinds of stimulus.

To research something means to find out about it. In this case you must call on as many resources as possible to acquire knowledge about your stimulus. You could use books, archive materials, film footage, the internet, museums, libraries, pictures, interview people, and call upon anything else that is appropriate to your stimulus and that will further your knowledge and understanding of it.

Your school or college library or resources centre will be a logical first port of call. If they don't have the relevant information, they will be able to help you source it from elsewhere.

Figure 7.1
The library will be able to help you find books and resources
Source: Photo Jacqueline Porteous.

Make sure that you keep all the information throughout the entire unit in one place as this will make it easy to write up your SWED (Supporting Written Evidence Document) on completion of the unit.

What should a SWEDE look like?

Like this . . .

Figure 7.2
Can you tell the difference between a SWED and a SWEDE?
Source: Photo Peter Gibbon.

What should a Unit 3 SWED look like?

The starting point for your SWED is likely to be a school exercise book or a small notebook where you can record everything you do connected with your Unit 3 piece. Initially it is where you will record everything that you research. It is important that you keep your individual notes on the process alongside a group's collective notes, as both of these will inevitably be used to create your final SWED. You will not have worked in isolation on devising your Unit 3 piece, although you may have taken on specific tasks in the preparation, and it is important that your SWED enables you to put the 'I' into the 'We' of the experience.

The extract from a notebook opposite indicates the starting point of some research into World War I medals. What you choose to research is a very personal thing and, because Unit 3 is such a creative unit, there are no hard-and-fast rules as to what or how you should research.

The examples given in this chapter follow similar themes but one stimulus is script-based and the other is not.

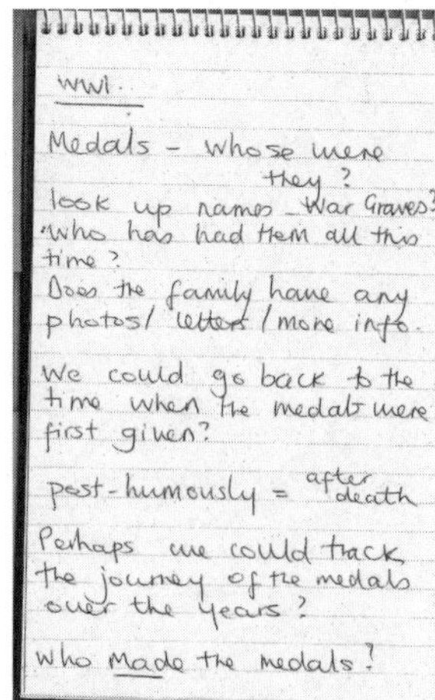

Figure 7.3
Keeping a notebook is a key tool for drama research
Source: Photo Jacqueline Porteous.

SCRIPT	STIMULUS
The Accrington Pals By Peter Whelan Written in 1981 Set between 1914 and 1916, this play tells the story of the Lancashire town of Accrington that lost almost all of its men in World War I	World War I 1 Some medals from soldiers who fought in the war 2 A poppy 3 Wilfred Owen's poem 'Anthem For Doomed Youth' 4 Women's call-up papers

Route 1

Your teacher could choose to use only the script with you. In other words, you take Peter Whelan's play *The Accrington Pals* and use that as a basis for devising your performance. We will discuss this in more detail later in the chapter.

Route 2

Your teacher could choose to use only the stimulus materials with you, delivering a series of workshops based around the four items suggested in the box above.

Route 3

Your teacher could choose to use both the script and the stimulus materials with you, giving you some choice in what you select to inform your performance.

Whichever route you choose, your starting point will have to be to research and explore the possibilities offered by the stimulus materials, be it a play or other materials.

The Examiner says:

There is an equal distribution of marks for each of the assessment elements of this unit and it is important that your response takes this into account. Your teacher as assessor will need to justify decisions made about marks awarded and these will be moderated against the agreed national standard for the unit. You need to ensure that you have the evidence in place and this does not simply mean that you are *outstanding* in the performance itself.

While this may be the case, your *outstanding* in the performance will earn you up to 15 marks, a quarter of the total. You need to plan and structure your response at every stage of the process, the performance and the evaluation of it if you are to access the higher bands of marks for the whole unit, not just one element of it in relation to the assessment criteria.

Here is the selection of four stimulus materials as suggested:

1.

Figure 7.4
Medals
Source: Photo Peter Gibbon

2.

Figure 7.5
Remembrance Poppies at Menin Gate, Ypres, Belgium

3.

ANTHEM FOR DOOMED YOUTH

What passing-bells for these who die as cattle?
Only the monstrous anger of the guns.
Only the stuttering rifles' rapid rattle
Can patter out their hasty orisons.
No mockeries now for them; no prayers nor bells;
Nor any voice of mourning save the choirs, –
The shrill, demented choirs of wailing shells;
And bugles calling for them from sad shires.
What candles may be held to speed them all?
Not in the hands of boys but in their eyes
Shall shine the holy glimmers of goodbyes.
The pallor of girls' brows shall be their pall;
Their flowers the tenderness of patient minds,
And each slow dusk a drawing-down of blinds.

September–October, 1917

Wilfred Owen

4.

A.F.W. 3030.

WOMEN'S ARMY AUXILIARY CORPS.

R. 20.

CALLING-UP NOTICE.

Miss / ~~Mrs.~~ C. E. Bridger

With reference to your enrolment for service in the Women's Army Auxiliary Corps you are hereby ordered to present yourself at A. Sqn. Stanhope Lines Marl. Aldershot on 7. November 1917.

Full directions for your journey are given below, and 2 railway warrants are enclosed.

You should bring all necessary underclothing with you, and your luggage should consist of a small handbag or parcel only; it is suggested that you provide yourself with a rug.

If for any unforeseen reason you are unable to travel on the day mentioned you should at once communicate with the Office given below.

C. F. N. MACREADY,
Adjutant General.

DIRECTIONS FOR JOURNEY.

You are to leave Richmond Station by the train leaving at 2.28 ~~and to travel to~~ Clapham Junc 2.43. ~~Station, at which you will arrive at~~ Train leaves Clapham Junc: * ~~You will be seen off at~~ 3.12. Arrives Aldershot 4.27. met at Aldershot ~~by~~ . If not met at the Station you should proceed to A. Sqn. Stanhope Lines Marl. Aldershot.

All further communications with regard to this notice should be addressed to the Divisional Officer. BARTLETT HOUSE BOW STREET.

(OFFICE STAMP).

* Strike out if no arrangements for seeing off are made.

(18) (74678) Wt. 25345/415 35,000 8-17 W B & L

Figure 7.6
A WAAC's call-up papers and travel documents
Source: www.militaryimages.net.

A really effective way of working is to divide tasks up among your group. For homework, each person in your group could agree to find something out for your next lesson so that you come to that session with more information that you can share. Another useful idea is to ask your drama teacher if you can have a space on the wall of the drama studio or classroom as a sort of 'drawing-board' so that you can pin up things as you collect them for all the group to see. This is also where you could display your rehearsal schedule and attendance register.

It is very important when you are working as a group that all communication is open and transparent for everyone to see, and a communal notice-board is one way of facilitating this.

Extension Activity

Create a notice-board for your group

- Don't put tasks off. If you think that this might be productive for your group, sort it out *now*. Pin up ideas, articles, photos, rehearsal schedules, attendance register, etc.

Let us begin by suggesting a few ways in which you might research and explore the four stimulus ideas.

1 *Medals*

- What was each medal for?
- Who did the medals belong to?
- Was he alive or dead when they were awarded?
- What happened to him?
- Where did he come from?
- Had he any family?
- If so, who?
- Who has the medals today?
- Are there any photographs connected with this person?
- Were they happy at war?

Eventually, as you begin to explore the dramatic possibilities of the information you research, you will find that your drama moves away from facts and becomes more fictitious as you begin to weave a story or plot around the stimulus. For example, you may decide that the owner of the medals had just learned that his wife had given birth to their first child, or that his father was seriously ill. You are trying to create tension and a plot that will engage your audience.

2 *Poppies*

- Look at the poem 'In Flanders Fields' by John McRae.
- Research the Poppy Factory and its history.

- Find out about Moina Bell Michael and Madame Guerin.
- Look at other events such as Holocaust Memorial Day.
- Look at the facts and statistics on the Royal British Legion site.
- November 2008 marked the ninetieth anniversary of the end of The Great War. Research some of the events that happened on that day.
- Can you interview any war veterans?
- Can you find any songs or music specifically written about war?

3 *'Anthem for Doomed Youth' by Wilfred Owen*

- Who was Wilfred Owen?
- Research his life. How old was he when he died? How did he die?
- Look at other war poets who were around at the same time as Owen.
- Analyse the poem. What does it mean? There is a lot written about this poem. Can you find out more about it?
- Could you dramatise the poem in some way?
- Could you create a soundscape to accompany the poem?

4 *Call-up papers for Miss Bridger*

- Find out more about the WAAC.
- Miss Bridger is to leave Richmond station. Can you create an improvised scene as she waits at the station for the train?
- What was happening in November 1917 in terms of the war?
- How does Miss Bridger feel about being called up?
- Where might she be sent to?
- Can you do a hot-seating exercise to explore her character?
- Improvise the scene when Miss Bridger arrives at Aldershot. What job might she typically expect to be doing?

The bullet points above provide just a few of the many ways that you could purposefully begin to research and explore these materials.

Practical activities such as these will allow your group to develop material for performance quickly and practically. You should take every opportunity you can to explore ideas practically, which is why the improvisation tasks will be really useful for you.

RESEARCHING AND EXPLORING A TEXT

- *The Accrington Pals* is based on a true story. Find out as much as you can about what happened in Accrington in World War I.

- Look at the issues of class within the play. Can you retell this story, focusing exclusively on the social, cultural and class issues?
- Peter Whelan talks about the impossible love of May and Tom. Explore their relationship further by doing some off-text improvisations.
- Research some of the songs that would have been sung by soldiers in World War I.
- Focusing primarily on May, retell her story, as if to a friend who wasn't there at the time.
- Take out all the scenes that are set at the front and explore the possibilities of linking these together without using the scenes back in Accrington.
- Improvise the scene when the people left in Accrington realise that almost all of their men have been killed.
- Consider other scripted source material. *Private Peaceful* by Simon Reade, for example, gives a vivid account of the last hours of a soldier about to be shot for cowardice and, in its structure, may give you ideas for your own piece based on the given stimulus.

HOW YOUR RESEARCH AND EXPLORATION IS ACTUALLY ASSESSED

This element of Unit 3 is assessed through the SWED (Supporting Written Evidence Document). In other words, you need to write down what you are doing to research and explore and what you actually find out that is relevant to your final piece. As we have already suggested in the Introduction to this book, a small notebook that you keep with you is a really practical way to do this so that you can take notes throughout this process. Here is an example of the sort of things you might record while researching and exploring.

WORKED EXAMPLE

This example from a SWED shows a student who has written about her character development. To talk about your own role is usually a very good starting point. Her character is called Holly, and in this extract she shows how she has developed her role and how she intends to interact with the other characters.

> *When my group started devising, I began to look at my use of language. I recognised the different ways Holly should react to each character and the effect this would have on me vocally. I developed*

particular ways of talking to each character. For example, when talking to Benjamin, I spoke as if speaking to a small child. I wanted to emphasise the way Holly perceives him as someone very fragile, who needs to be taken care of. I decided it should contrast with how I spoke to George, which was more forceful, and angry. This showed different sides to my character, and helped to formulate a specific relationship with each character. I also looked at the use of proxemics. I felt that the proxemics said a great deal about my relationship with Benjamin. I showed my affection for him by standing or sitting close to him, but I was unable to touch him, as I knew he would have reacted badly. I used proxemics to show my status in relation to George. During arguments, we often changed levels to show who had the 'upper hand'.

When developing my first scene, I considered how I wanted the audience to first perceive my character. I decided I wanted to make an impact, so I entered onto the stage whilst having an argument with my husband. I wanted to make it obvious that Holly is miserable, but I left it ambiguous as to why, because I wanted the audience to unravel the reason as the play went along. I wanted Holly to appear as a strong character, as she is not scared to have an argument with George, and also as very caring, as they are arguing about Benjamin. (287 words)

Note how the student has recorded the word count at the end of this contribution to her SWED. This is important, as the word limit set by the Examination Board is the maximum allowed, and, by keeping a total as you go along, you can get a sense of how balanced your SWED is likely to be across the suggested elements for inclusion.

Extension Activity

Considering the word count

- Look again at the extract from the SWED. It comprises 287 words.
- Rewrite it so that it includes the same information but aim to do this in no more than 250 words, giving you an extra 37 words to play with in other sections of the SWED.

8 Development and structure

The focus of this chapter is to show a range of ways in which you could develop and structure your response to the stimulus that your teacher gives you. Unit 3 is marked out of a total of 60 marks which is scaled down to give 40 per cent of the A2 overall, 20 per cent of the A level percentage. A quarter of the available marks are given for your development and structure (i.e. 15 marks out of 60).

An outstanding contribution to development and structure is described in the specification as follows:

> Students demonstrate an outstanding involvement in the developmental process with a creative and imaginative input that has a far-reaching benefit to both their own work and the work of others.

Once you have your stimulus in place, be it a scripted play or a devised piece, you will start to develop and structure it. Much of this work happens instinctively as you and the other people in your group have ideas that you want to try out, and of course the date of your performance, usually a couple of months ahead, gives you something to constantly aim for. How you develop and structure your piece will vary depending on many factors:

- How creative you are
- How imaginative you are
- How good you are at recognising dramatic potential
- If you recognise when something isn't working
- If you are well organised
- How well you manage your time
- Whether you are a positive or a negative thinker
- Whether you are able to move things forward
- If you tend to reject ideas instead of trying them out
- Whether you are flexible
- Whether you take risks
- Whether you can turn your ideas into practical drama

- Whether you have seen enough live theatre to influence your work
- Whether you know enough about your chosen practitioner/genre to develop your drama effectively
- Whether you are sufficiently aware of your audience so that your piece is relevant and appropriate to them
- Whether you are able to use all that you learned in the AS year to help develop this piece.

It is impossible to dictate or even speculate how any group might develop their devised drama from a given starting point. Whether you are part of a large group or a small group, your teacher may well give you all the same stimulus and yet it is certain that you will end up with very different performance pieces. This is the challenge and the joy of creating your own performance, be it from a script or a different form of stimulus. In this chapter we will show some of the ways you might develop and structure a devised response to a given script and a given stimulus.

SCRIPT

The Crucible

By Arthur Miller

Written in 1953

Set in Salem, Massachusetts

This play tells the story of the small town of Salem, the witch trials that took place there, and John Proctor and his wife Elizabeth and how they struggle to clear their name in the face of unfounded allegations and hysteria.

STIMULUS

Article describing McCarthyism in America in the early 1950s

The story of the Witches of Warboys

Guardian article written in 2008 about a man who was wrongly accused of murder

DEVELOPING THE SCRIPT

It goes without saying that if you are using a script, you must know it extremely well. It would be naive to think that *The Crucible* is just a play about witches; this would lead to a piece of drama that was superficial and lacking in depth. Arthur Miller wrote *The Crucible* in response to anti-communist feelings that were prevalent in America in the 1950s. Senator John McCarthy and other politicians led a high-scale investigation to oust people who had any communist leanings or beliefs. Some people likened this to a witch-hunt, but that is really a figure of speech. However, it is important to know the historical background to the play, and this is certainly something you would need to write about in your SWED.

The next section shows some of the ways you could develop and structure your work based on this particular script. There are an infinite number of directions it could take, and these are just a few of them.

Route 1

Look at the play from the point of view of one character and reconstruct the script so that everything is seen from that character's point of view. For example, Abigail Williams is a strong, feisty and manipulative character. Structure your piece to show that Abigail was wronged, that in fact John Proctor seduced her. You could also develop a scene showing that when she worked for Elizabeth Proctor she was not treated fairly, giving her reason to dislike Elizabeth. You could try to show that people fall under Abigail's spell as if they are frightened of her.

Route 2

Choose a theme from the play. Justice would work well. Select all the extracts from the text that look at justice and the law. Using these extracts, piece together a version of the play that follows the same plot as *The Crucible* but which focuses particularly on justice and the law.

Route 3

Focus on the parts from the play where some people are accusing others. As you act out these scenes, you could juxtapose your play with background projections showing parallel situations that occurred in the McCarthy enquiries or of stories from around the world when people have been wrongly accused of doing things. You could call this piece 'Accused'.

Route 4

You may decide that the young women and girls in the town of Salem are all afraid of Abigail and that she somehow controls them. You want to show this by having the young women represented as pawns in a game of chess where Abigail moves them around like puppets, or chess pieces. Your floor, or floor cloth, could be painted in black and white squares which in itself would be enough to show your audience that you are suggesting a game of chess.

Route 5

You could structure your performance in such a way that it resembled a fight between Abigail and Elizabeth. The piece could follow a series of 'rounds' rather like a boxing match with a bell ringing periodically to signal the end of that particular round. In between the 'rounds' you could use thought-tracking to reveal what characters were thinking or you could have other characters from the piece commenting on what they had just witnessed as if from the sides of the boxing ring. You could even make your piece more Brechtian and use placards, encouraging characters, showing scores as well as songs in between each 'round'.

When travesty becomes tragedy (*The Guardian*)

- Trial by tabloid and police errors framed Colin Stagg for the murder of Rachel Nickell, while Robert Napper went free

There are many victims in a single murder. The family and friends of the person killed have to spend the rest of their lives with that shadow forever in the background. Often, too, the family of the killer, shocked by the act carried out by someone they loved, find their lives permanently blighted by guilt and shame. And, occasionally, but still too often, there is the person wrongly accused of the *crime*.

The *Rachel Nickell* case, which finally reached its conclusion at the Old Bailey on Thursday, more than 16 years after she was killed in front of her two-year-old son on Wimbledon Common, is one with all too many victims: her partner and father of their child, Andre Hanscombe; that young son, who had to witness the murder; her family and many friends. But there was an additional victim in *Colin Stagg*, the 27th person arrested by *police* in their investigation and the first one to go to the Old Bailey and face trial for the murder back in 1994. Now, with the conviction of the real killer, *Robert Napper*, he has his *formal vindication*.

Stagg was fortunate in that the judge in the original case, Mr Justice Ognall, was robust and self-confident enough to see the case against him for what it was – a mishmash of suppositions and mild coincidences, sprinkled with some fanciful psychological speculation. Stagg was in jail for 13 months while he awaited trial. Even after he was freed, back in 1994, the innuendos continued, with some members of the press clearly still anxious to tar him with the brush of the 'man who got away with murder'.

To his great credit, Stagg has always said that the real victims in this whole sorry saga are Rachel and her family. What he has suffered, with all the graffiti on his walls, all the snooping on his life and love affairs by a suspicious press, is far less, he has said, than the loss of someone so loved. But that should not detract from the fact that, but for the intervention of the judge, he could well only now be coming out of jail after being convicted by a jury which found itself bamboozled by the evidence and under pressure to satisfy public demand to solve such a notorious crime.

Stagg has not blamed the detectives in the case. They were under enormous pressure, as evidenced by the fact that so many people were arrested – 13 in the first month – for the crime. When the murder took place, the *criminal justice* system was just coming to terms with a catalogue of miscarriages of justice. In 1991, the *Birmingham Six* had finally been released and two years before that, *the Guildford Four*. The very week that Rachel Nickell was killed, a high-profile appeal, that of *the Darvell brothers*, who had been wrongly convicted of a murder in Swansea, was being heard. They, too, might have been regarded as 'the local weirdos', and their successful appeal should have been yet another alarm bell reminding the police, the prosecution services and the media that real-life murder investigations are not as neat and simple as a television drama.

This was not a case where evidence was planted or confessions invented, as in the old days. This was incompetence not corruption. It came at a time when 'psychological profiling' – as portrayed in the television series, *Cracker*, which started in 1993, the year before Stagg appeared in court – was seen as a magic solution to a tricky case rather than just a useful potential aid.

There will be many questions for the senior ranks of the police, the prosecution services and the psychological profilers to answer. However, the case is another reminder that the 'local weirdo', who may seem to be the likeliest suspect, can all too often be another victim.

DEVELOPING AND STRUCTURING FROM THE STIMULUS MATERIALS

You could decide to use all three of these given ideas: McCarthyism, The Witches of Warboys story, and the newspaper article about Colin Stagg. Alternatively, you might choose to use just one of the ideas and develop that. Realistically, you need to consider how much material you need to work with in order to develop a performance that lasts for up to 20 minutes, depending on the size of your performance group. The next section shows some of the ways you could develop and structure your work based on one or more of these stimulus ideas. There are an infinite number of directions it could take, and these are just a few of them.

Route 1

Create your own devised drama that centres around people being accused of doing something they haven't done. How do they react? What happens to them? Do they have a voice? Who represents them? What time period is the piece set in? What is the outcome? Does justice prevail? Are some people guilty of the accused crime? Do they get away with it or do they caught?

Route 2

Try to create a historical piece in the same way Miller wrote *The Crucible*. Base the plot of your piece around the story of the Witches of Warboys. Spend time on character development. Research more about the Throckmortons. Find out facts and statistics about Warboys itself. Look for other stories about towns and villages in the late 1500s so that you can include more factual information and details in your own piece.

Route 3

Imagine you live in the town where someone has recently been murdered. Try to create all the people who may have known the victim (e.g. teachers, shopkeepers, the postman, hairdresser, window cleaner, friends in the local pub, car mechanic). There would be lots of opportunities for people in your group to multi-role, which can be an effective way of demonstrating your acting skills. Imagine that they all have a story to tell about the victim. Find ways of linking their stories so that they run into each other.

Perhaps the stories begin to change in tone after people's initial response and shock to the news that someone in their town has been murdered. Show, as the 'sound bites' progress, how they can change and become distorted so that people (the audience) begin to believe different things about the victim from the sentiments first expressed. This piece could reflect the power of the media and how they can control audience responses to events.

HOW THIS ASSESSMENT ELEMENT IS ASSESSED

Your teacher will assess how well you develop and structure your piece. He or she will listen in to your many conversations and discussions while you are shaping and selecting materials. He or she will notice when you miss rehearsals, when you encourage and support others, and will have an overview of your contribution to the piece overall. Your teacher will record your contribution to the development of the piece at regular intervals during the process in order to form an opinion about your overall contribution against the assessment criteria.

WORKED EXAMPLE

Consider the extract below which is from a student's SWED. It shows how the student began to structure and develop the stimulus based on the story of the Witches of Warboys.

> *The stimulus we received was an extract from a book about crime and punishment in the sixteenth century. It outlines a case of a village elder who was accused of witchcraft, after she had cared for a family of successful landowners. She, along with her family were hanged in the winter of 1593 for accepting the fact they were witches. If Alice Samuel (the accused) refused to say aloud the clause (claiming she was a witch), then it would be thought she was guilty anyway.*
>
> *We read the stimulus aloud, as a group, and began to generate ideas about the themes within it. Examples of the themes we thought of were: power, witchcraft, corruption, injustice, punishment and isolation. After this, we discussed how we believed we might make a decision based on the stimulus, in terms of our own work. We decided that a period piece (i.e. that of a drama based*

in an historical timeframe) would suit us as a group very well. This was partly due to our great enjoyment with our Unit 2 performance, which was a period-piece (Our Country's Good) *and partly as we felt it would be more challenging than a modern-day piece.*

So, in effect, we used the plot of the stimulus as the backbone for our own drama. We had a witch who was wrongly accused of witchcraft and consequently hanged. However, we did make our piece more interesting and 'colourful' by adding other elements, such as affairs, secrets, corruption in society and betrayal in families. Examples would be the fact that the witch's own sister, Isabel, is the one who has the real power in our tale, as she is the one who puts Alice forward as a witch.

(286 words)

Later on, this student gives a detailed and very effective account of how the group had structured one of their scenes. There is clear evidence here of creativity.

Another way in which the group developed the stimulus or explored it, was by taking the main gist of it – i.e. 'Alice Samuel – innocent or guilty?' and turning it into a news story. Half of us argued that Alice was guilty; a threat to the village and so must be hanged for her selfish, evil behaviour. The other half of us opposed this, and claimed that she was simply being misunderstood and actually was totally innocent.

Through carrying out this relatively simple yet effective creative activity, we had another idea for a scene in our performance – that of the village council. We felt it would be very interesting to put together a scene centred around a village council meeting. This is because we believed that the audience would be able to hear both sides of the argument, as to whether Alice was guilty or not: and make their own minds up.

(150 words)

You may find it frustrating that your teacher is not always present when you come up with imaginative ideas or you are the one that always seems to move your group forward. Most drama teachers do seem able to tell what is happening from quite a distance, but it is always worth telling them exactly what you have done if you are in any doubt. You can of course discuss this with your teacher, but it is probably much more effective to use your SWED as the obvious place to record what you did. As long as you are always honest when acknowledging ideas from others, as well as about what you contributed, your SWED will form important evidence for all elements of this unit.

Extension Activity

The use of language

- Look again at the two SWED extracts overleaf. Consider how effectively the student uses the language of drama and theatre and consider whether there are words or phrases missing from the extracts that you might expect to see here.
- Rewrite the two extracts to include the words or phrases and see if you can reduce the total word count across both extracts by 50 words.

9 Performance

The focus of this chapter is to show a range of ways in which you can approach your Unit 3 performance and how you can maximise the marks available to you.

- Unit 3 is marked out of a total of 60 marks which is scaled down to give 40 per cent of the A2 overall, or 20 per cent of the A level percentage.
- A quarter of the available marks for this unit are given for your actual performance (i.e. 15 marks out of 60).

Outstanding performance work is described in the specification as follows:

> Students demonstrate outstanding skills within the compass of their chosen role or roles within the assessed performance. Their contribution to the performance comprehensively communicates their intentions to the audience.

Once you have completed your actual performance, you will be approximately 85 per cent of the way through Unit 3. However, the performance itself is not the end of the unit. You still have the evaluation of the performance to complete which will be written up in your SWED. As you are evaluating the process as well as the performance, some of the evaluation will already be completed.

The obvious starting point for your Unit 3 performance is to look back and reflect upon your Unit 2 performance from the AS year. Assuming you chose to act – be assessed as a Performance candidate in Unit 2 – you will have performed in a group piece and presented either a monologue or a duologue for section A.

Just to remind you, the four elements that are assessed for Unit 2 performances are:

- Vocal skills
- Movement skills

- Characterisation
- Communication.

Although these four areas are not named separately for your Unit 3 performance, it would be wise to assume that they will still count towards an outstanding performance. The criteria refer to 'skills' and 'communication'.

If you are a Performance candidate, *skills* for Unit 3 could mean:

- The clarity of your voice
- Using appropriate tone of voice
- Use of pauses
- Projection and volume of your voice
- Pace – how quickly you speak and how well judged your interjections are
- Intonation in your voice – do you communicate through your tone of voice as well as in what you say?
- Use of gesture
- Controlled and purposeful movements
- Maintaining stillness and poise when required
- Facial expressions
- Considered use of proxemics
- Consistent use of accent or an assumed voice if you choose to use one
- Considered characterisation that shows an understanding of your role/s
- Consistency in your characterisation
- Sympathetic character portrayal within the context of the piece
- An ease and rapport with other members of your company/cast
- An awareness of your audience and their response
- An awareness of others on stage with you
- A sense that you are 'listening' to others on stage, and responding and reacting accordingly.

This is not a definitive list, but it does go some way towards defining the term 'skills' so that you can see how challenging it is to have an outstanding command of so many different things.

In the Unit 2 assessment criteria for Design candidates there were separate skills listed, such as:

- Use of materials and equipment
- Realisation of design
- Design documentation
- Written design concept.

If you are a Design candidate, *skills* for Unit 3 could mean:

- You handle your chosen media with confidence (e.g. a lighting board, sound equipment), and you have the necessary skills to create imaginative and appropriate props.
- You can not only 'make' things, you know how to apply them effectively to the group's chosen piece (e.g. costumes are original and appropriate, they enhance the characters and make the production easier to understand).
- Your technical skills are well advanced, you know how to use your chosen skill to great effect and are an integral part of the group. Your designs complement and enhance the production; they do not overpower it nor are underwhelmed by it.
- You are competent, comfortable and proficient in the use of your chosen skill. It would not be sensible to do something for the first time at this level of study.
- You are able to demonstrate the stages you went through as you developed your chosen skill throughout the devising/rehearsing process. Your documentation is skilfully drawn up (e.g. if you are offering sound, you can produce cue sheets and midi-files etc as appropriate to the production).
- Design students will have to show their research and exploration and evaluation of what they have done in the SWED, the same as everyone else.

By this stage of the course, you should know whether you feel more comfortable and confident working with a script or working with a given stimulus. The script example given in this chapter is *King Lear*, which is a very long play – at least three hours' running time. Assuming you are working in a group of four students, you are going to end up with a running time of about 20 minutes. Deconstructing or reducing the script to this playing time is in itself time consuming; however, it offers many advantages. Before you can cut or edit the script, you will need to know the complete version well, and this means that you will have a wealth of material to use in your actual performance. As a performer, your characters will be extremely well developed and you will know a great deal about their backgrounds, motives and traits. As long as you can bring all this knowledge to your performance, it will stand you in good stead to communicate this to your audience. As a Design candidate, similarly, you will have the complete play to base your decisions on, so that your design may take things into account that can help demonstrate your wider knowledge and understanding.

What you choose to demonstrate in performance is a very personal thing, and, because Unit 3 is such a creative unit, there are no hard-and-fast rules as to the route you choose to demonstrate your skills in performance.

The examples given in this chapter show how the script of *King Lear* may be used in its own right or how some of the themes and issues in this play could be used to develop a devised piece. Of course, it is also possible to combine some of the script with some devised work.

SCRIPT	STIMULUS
King Lear by William Shakespeare Written in 1605 This play tells the story of how King Lear bequeaths all his land and belongings to his three daughters and what befalls him afterwards.	Parent–child relationships Sibling rivalry Tests of loyalty and love Parallel stories that reflect upon each other Lies, deceit and disguise

The examples outlined below assume a group of three students. The minimum performance time for this unit is 15 minutes, and for a group of three this would be the sensible time limit to aim for. We would certainly suggest no more than 20 minutes maximum for three candidates.

Using only the script, you could:

- Focus only on Lear, Goneril and Cordelia to show how differently their relationships function with their father.
- Focus on father–child relationships. Having one performer play the role of both Lear and Gloucester, show how this father figure treats his children. The other two performers could play Goneril, Regan, Cordelia, and Edgar and Edmund. This may sound quite confusing but multi-roling can be a most effective way of showing off your skills. You could use simple costume changes or vocal changes to name several obvious ways to portray different characters.
- You could take one of the major themes in the play and develop that. A fascinating theme to explore would be the notion of 'sight' and 'seeing'. When Lear has his eyesight he cannot see what is happening in front of his nose. When he loses his sight he eventually sees how his daughters have deceived him. Similarly, Gloucester has his eyes gouged out before he sees things clearly. There are so many references to sight and seeing in the play that it would not be difficult to re-create a 15-minute piece based on this alone.

If you wanted to work from a stimulus through using ideas from *King Lear* as outlined in the stimulus box above, you could:

- Create a play where a parent favours one child over another. Stepchildren may be an effective way of showing this and would reflect many families today.
- Create a scenario where one or more siblings gang up on the third sibling. This could be quite sinister and there may well be stories you could find from news articles about cases where this has actually happened.
- *King Lear* has a superb subplot that runs alongside the main plot. Using this structure as a stimulus in its own right, devise a play that has two distinctive strands to it that eventually converge.
- Although it is a simplistic description of *King Lear*, you could say that the play is based on lies, deceit and disguise. Create a piece of your own that uses these three dramatic elements on which to structure your play.

Essentially, your performance in this unit, be it as performer or designer, needs to be as well researched, rehearsed and executed as you can possibly make it. Whatever skill you are offering, you will be assessed as an individual within your group.

This is also the last time that you will do performance work or practical work that is formally assessed on your A2 course, so it is well worth giving it everything you possibly can.

10 Evaluation

The focus of this chapter is to show a range of ways in which you might evaluate the stimulus your teacher gives you.

- Unit 3 is marked out of a total of 60 marks which is scaled down to give 40 per cent of the A2 overall, 20 per cent of the A level.
- A quarter of the available marks are given for your evaluation (i.e. 15 marks out of 60).

Outstanding evaluation is described in the specification as follows:

> Students produce an outstanding evaluation of the process and performance. Perceptive links are made between the influence of research, developmental activity and the performance, taking significant note of the involvement of self and appreciative contribution of others.

What does it mean to evaluate something? Put simply, to evaluate something means to weigh it up carefully and reflect. You need to consider the strengths and weaknesses of the process and the performance, and to produce a balanced and thoughtful response to what you and your group did.

We regularly evaluate things while we are doing them and in drama this is usually done verbally (e.g. 'It would be better if you stood there when you said that line because . . .'). In effect, this is an evaluative comment. You are

making a judgement that something could be improved if it was done in a different way. It is essential that all these moments are jotted down in your working notebook as you prepare, create and rehearse your Unit 3 piece.

All your actual evidence must be recorded in your SWED. Thus, although, many of your thoughts and observations will be heard by your teacher and by the others in your group, you must ensure that you write things down in order for them to be formally assessed. In Chapter 11 that describes how to use the SWED, you are reminded that the SWED must not exceed 3,500 words. Given that two of the four assessed areas are evidenced through the SWED, we suggest you use about half of the available word count to cover your evaluation i.e. 1,750 words.

The SWED is 3,500 words maximum

Research and exploration = 1,750	Evaluation = 1,750 words
	You might then write 875 words evaluating the process
	And you might write 875 words evaluating the performance

Although it seems clinical to divide up the word count in this way, it does ensure that you achieve a balance between the two areas. It is also a good check for you to ensure that you are addressing all the areas that are stated in the specification and in the assessment criteria.

The two worked examples below are both exactly 850 words long, and each one evaluates the process (research and exploration) and the performance respectively.

WORKED EXAMPLE

Evaluating the process (research and exploration) of a Unit 3 piece

As a group, we had different ideas about how various scenes should be presented. An example would be the opening scene. Some of us felt that a sudden, sharp start would begin the play with strong dramatic impact. Others believed that a calmer, quieter start would be more fitting with the church setting. After we had acted out the start in the two ways, we took the group decision that to start the play with four of us entering the studio singing, walking through the audience, and the vicar standing on the staging in front of the audience, would be the best possible method.

As well as the example above, another way in which we developed our drama was when we were discussing the overall plot of the play. At times, some of us 'dried up' and ran out of ideas. What was helpful was that someone in the group always had ideas to 'put into the pot'. For instance, we were unsure how to build in the adulterous relationship between the vicar and Lady Throckmorton. After thinking up different scenes that may show this, someone in the group suggested that the two people actually acting these characters ought to explore the relationship using improvisation. This worked wonders on this occasion, and everyone else watching contributed ideas that helped the two actors and significantly moved the process forward. It was so helpful as the scenes end up much more naturalistic and fluid.

By allocating each other different research-based tasks, we were able to get the most out of our time. This is because, instead of six different tasks being done by one person, each of us had just one. For this reason, the next day, we had completed a huge amount of research into various areas such as the type of language used at the time, popular seventeenth-century names (mentioned above), costume ideas and the attitude towards witches in England at this period in time.

Another decision we made as a group when we were working on a scene between about three of us was that anyone could stop the action and suggest ways in which it could be improved. For instance, 'I think you ought to say this instead of that because it portrays a feeling of . . .', or 'try walking this way, rather than like this, because it shows that you are . . .'.

After we began to draft out scenes that Alice's ghost was to be involved in, as a group, we felt that actually this did not work. Instead, we thought if she became Alice's sister, who had been killed in another village for witchcraft, it would be smoother. This is because she could narrate throughout the play and act almost as the audience's curiosity – as if she wants to get the play to continue, so she can find out more about how her sister lives her life. Put simply, Alice's sister's ghost became a tool to link the play together and move the plot on. This is often referred to as a framing device.

Throughout the process, we constantly discussed the development of our play. Rather than making decisions in twos or threes, where possible, we tried to make choices as a complete group – of course this was not always efficient at every stage of the process.

One of the most memorable and indeed significant discussions we had was when we decided the plot of the play. Naturally, we all had many ideas and it can be tempting just to focus on the inclusion of your own ideas, although this may not be the best thing. Through careful negotiation and compromise, we feel we got a plot which satisfied the needs of the group as a whole. There were occasions when we felt changes had to be made. Perhaps the most significant of these was when we deemed it inappropriate and soap-like for William Throckmorton (aged approximately 45) to have a relationship with Mary (his daughter's friend) aged approximately 20.

On a purely practical level, Charlotte and I attempted to move the process on day-to-day by putting together a schedule. This was distributed to all in the group. As well as this, Becky and I set up a production notice-board, which we all felt would help communication as a whole. The thinking behind it was to have a 'communal area' where all production-related issues could be aired. For instance, instead of designing a particular costume or prop individually and working from our own initiative, we could draft it out, put it up on the board, and people could annotate over it – so all decisions could be group decisions.

We felt, during rehearsals that certain parts of the plot were not put across clearly enough for our audience. For this reason, we felt putting in a scene where all the village community could talk about village life and discuss various characters within it, would solve this. After we discussed this, we decided that instead of all those in the village talking as one large gathering, we should split them up. This would show various friendship groups and relations. (850 words)

WORKED EXAMPLE

Evaluating the performance of a Unit 3 piece

Throughout the devising process, we never lost sight of the fact that we were aiming towards a performance with a live audience.

About two weeks before our actual performance exam, we began to show our play to classes in school. This proved invaluable as we could try things out and almost instantly, we felt they didn't work or more importantly we asked our 'trial' audiences for feedback which at times was blunt and disarmingly honest!

We felt sure that using a thrust stage would be extremely advantageous, as it would involve the audience and get them in on the action. This proved to be very effective in performance. By having a thrust stage, we were able to carry the action downstage and right out to our audience, and so get more out of our fairly limited space. Also, we had the chance to explore the status of different characters. For instance, the vicar would be on the rostra stage at the back of the thrust, whereas the congregation would be kneeling down at the foot of the staging – the status would therefore be clearer, than if everyone was on one level.

In terms of showing status, costume was a fantastic resource. This is because those in the village with a higher social standing wore grander clothes, as did the elders. This was especially helpful in the scene when the villagers met together to discuss the fate of Alice, as those with more authority in the village could be easily distinguished from those with lesser 'say' over matters. We knew that by careful costume choices our characters would be visually very recognisable to the audience in terms of social standing and position.

We wanted to make the audience feel 'part of the action' and not as if they were passively 'watching a play'. For this reason, the small studio space and thrust stage worked really well for us with audience members telling us they felt complicit in much of the action. Initially, we thought a traverse set-up would work well, but many of us preferred the security of thrust staging. We also felt that this would allow us to explore the use of a church-setting more fully.

I felt that the lighting in our performance was particularly effective and the key technical aspect which communicated our intentions and ideas to the audience. This is because we concentrated on creating lighting states that effectively reflected the mood and atmosphere of the situation. For instance, in the first scene, we lit the set in such a way as to create a sombre and 'gloomy' mood. This was achieved through unfocused ('hazy') general washes across the set in a dim, white-yellow colour. I think it was especially helpful in engaging our audience from the outset as it instantly put them in the 'right frame of mind' from the minute they took their seats, as we didn't use the traditional, rather un-naturalistic 'fade down houselights, fade up stage lights' method.

Another example of when we got the most out of our lighting resources would be with after the hanging of Alice – the 'witch' at the end of our play. This is because the lighting was used in such a way to focus the attention of the audience on the harshness of her situation – very white, cold colours. It was clear that the starkness of this had quite a shocking effect on some of the audience. However, after she had been hanged, the lights faded out fairly slowly – perhaps over five or six seconds. This really reinforced just how unfortunate and desperate Alice's situation was: there was no hope for her.

We had a very real concern that a modern-day audience might just perceive our piece as a play about witches. We asked the History Department how they taught this issue with regards to women in the Middle Ages being accused of witchcraft and inevitably sentenced to death. It appeared that there was still some sense that witches were 'silly women' who deserved all they got. We also read *The Crucible* by Arthur Miller to see how he had portrayed the women of that time.

We considered using both the programme and/or back projections to help inform our audience about the injustice of what had happened historically. However, some of our group felt that this was a cop out and that the performance itself should convey the fact that innocent women (and occasionally men) had been sentenced to death. Overall, I think we conveyed this very successfully in our performance. Early feedback from our 'trial' audiences said that people had wanted to call out and stop the hanging just before the rope was dropped. This was what we had wanted to create, and we likened it to the moment in *Romeo and Juliet* when the audience want to stop Romeo thinking that Juliet really is dead.

In conclusion, our performance was thoroughly researched, rehearsed and performed with confidence and honesty. We made many changes and improvements throughout the process which meant that the performance itself was as good as we could get it. (850 words)

These examples give an honest account of how a student has been involved in a Unit 3 devised piece and how they have reflected on the experience. There is definitely a feeling that they have made lots of notes as they have gone along and not written this up long after the event has faded from their memory!

There are lots of other things they could have done to present it differently and it is worth looking at the ideas given in Chapter 11 on SWED to see not only the suggestions given there but also to be aware that continuous written prose such as this example is not the only way of doing it.

11 The Supporting Written Evidence Document [SWED]

The SWED accounts for 50 per cent of the available marks for Unit 3. Here is a reminder of how the four available elements are assessed:

- Research and exploration is assessed through the SWED
- Development and structure is assessed by your teacher
- The performance is assessed by your teacher
- Your evaluation of the whole unit is assessed through the SWED.

All these elements are then subject to moderation which means that your work is sent off to the awarding body (Edexcel) to make sure that your centre's marks are in line with the national standard.

It says in the specification that the SWED should address the following questions:

1. How is the initial material being researched and developed at significant stages during the process of creating drama?
2. How effectively are you personally exploring and developing your role(s)?
3. How did you and your group explore the possibilities of form, structure and performance style?
4. How did the work of established and recognised theatre practitioners, and/or the work of live theatre, influence the way in which your devised response developed?
5. How successfully did your final performance communicate your aims and intentions for the piece to your audience?
6. How effectively did the social, cultural, historical/political context of the piece communicate to your audience?

These questions are open-ended and can apply equally to Performance students as well as to Design students. As there are a maximum of 3,500 words available for the SWED, including labelling of sketches, diagrams and photos, it is worth considering how you might divide up the word count.

Route 1

Research and development is worth half the marks available for the SWED so I will write half the word count (1,750 words) under this heading, and evaluation is worth the other half of the marks available, so I will write half the word count (1,750 words) under this heading which gives a total of 3,500 words.

Route 2

There are six areas I need to cover (see questions opposite or page 42 of the specification), so I will address both research and exploration and evaluation together, allocating approximately 580 words to each of the six questions.

Route 3

You could take research and evaluation on its own and address the six questions, allocating approximately 290 words to each of the questions, then write about evaluation addressing each of the six questions, allocating another 290 to each question, giving a total of 3,500 words (3,480 with 20 to spare).

Route 4

You could use a lot of sketches, diagrams and/or photos which are well labelled, justifying decisions made by your group as you progressed towards your final performance. This certainly seems a sensible route for Design candidates to take (e.g. as you label lighting plots or justify fabric and costume decisions).

You may choose to use around 1,000 words in a more creative way such as relevant labelling and then ensure that in the remaining 2,500 words you address the six questions that the specification says should be included in the SWED.

Route 5

Under evaluation, you may allocate 1,750 words as stated in Route 1 but then split that into your evaluation of the *process* and your evaluation of the *performance*, which would mean:

- Process evaluation = 875 words
- Performance evaluation = 875 words.

There are two important factors to remember:

1. You need to cover the necessary areas in a maximum of 3,500 words
2. QWC – The quality of your written communication matters.

You should be using drama-specific terminology in a range of contexts.

You should be able to analyse, reflect and evaluate the impact of decisions that were made and the effect they had on the final performance and your audience and write about them in an accurate and relevant way. Although QWC is not specifically assessed in Unit 3, it is in Unit 4, so it is in your own interests to be getting it right now.

We also think it matters in all contexts.

WRITING AS AN INDIVIDUAL WHILE WORKING ON A GROUP PROJECT

Your SWED is written on your own, and you are assessed as an individual. However, you will have worked as part of a group which can make it quite difficult to be clear about your own contribution. You must always be honest about what you did, and what others in your group did. Whenever you refer to other members of your group be certain that you are mentioning them in a relevant and positive light. There are no marks awarded for irrelevant comments such as: 'Naufel was always late for rehearsals and often rejected other people's ideas.' This may be true, but there is really nothing to be gained from this within your own SWED. However, it may be much more helpful to say, 'Morag steered us away from using pre-recorded sound effects and helped us create sounds using our own voices as well as clapping and stamping. On reflection, this was much more powerful as it allowed us to show a wider range of vocal skills and many audience members commented on how effective they thought it was.'

Try to avoid using negative sentences and instead think of rephrasing things to turn them into positive, evaluative comments that show you have learnt something.

- ✗ We argued about. . . .
- ✗ Peter was absent a lot.
- ✗ We spent three weeks on this idea before abandoning it and starting again. . . .
- ✗ We couldn't agree on the style of. . . .
- ✗ If we had had more time we would have. . . .
- ✓ In selecting materials, we also had the difficult task of discarding some of our earlier ideas. We did this by. . . .
- ✓ In the initial stages of research we worked most effectively when. . . .
- ✓ We found this effective because. . . .
- ✓ We preferred to use ABC because. . . .
- ✓ The Brechtian style allowed us to communicate the terror of the piece; this seemed more appropriate than. . . .
- ✓ We knew our audience were unlikely to have experienced anything like this within our own culture and times; however, historically we felt they could empathise with the characters, if not their situation.

The most important factor when making bold statements about what you did is to be able to justify why and how you did it. Words such as 'because' and 'for example' are key to justifying what you want to say.

Finally, see the SWED as an ongoing document that is compiled throughout the process and completed after the performance. It shouldn't be onerous and it isn't a document written from memory. It is a lively, vibrant account of how you created your Unit 3 piece.

OVERVIEW OF UNIT 4

PART III

This is your opportunity to demonstrate skills in a formal written examination environment, drawing on all of your previous experience in the AS year and your current experience in Unit 3. Your aim in this unit is to respond to a text as if you were the director and to respond to a live performance of a play as an informed member of the audience.

In Unit 3, your teacher is your examiner and assesses your contribution to devising against an agreed national standard of work for the unit. In Unit 4, your responses to the questions will be marked by an examiner who is appointed by the Examination Board and who will assess your work in relation to the agreed national standard for this unit. The knowledge and understanding you have gained throughout the course so far can now be applied to demonstrate your understanding of the work of the director in the theatre.

ASSESSMENT OBJECTIVES FOR UNIT 4

- **AO2**: Demonstrate knowledge and understanding of practical and theoretical aspects of drama and theatre using appropriate terminology.
- **AO3**: Interpret plays from different periods and genres.
- **AO4**: Make critical and evaluative judgements of live theatre.

There are three sections in this unit. In sections A and B, you take the role of director of a production of the chosen play and in section C you are responding to a play in performance as an informed member of the audience.

The text for sections A and B is one from a choice of three stipulated by the Examination Board and your teacher will be key in guiding you towards the text which he or she feels will enable you to access the marks for this unit. It is likely that your centre will study the same text over a number of years and that all groups in your centre will focus on the same text.

The texts for Unit 4 are:

- *Lysistrata* by Aristophanes
- *Doctor Faustus* by Christopher Marlowe
- *Woyzeck* by Georg Buchner.

Extension Activity

Overview of Texts for Unit 4

Find out what you can about the three Unit 4 texts and the playwrights. Compile some notes on one of the plays – possibly in pairs – to present to your group on a day to be agreed with your teacher. Your presentation should last for approximately 20 minutes and should include information on:

- The playwright
- Social conditions of the time the play was written
- Theatrical conventions of the time the play was first performed
- The plot and structure of the play itself.

The mark breakdown for section A and section B is as follows:

- Section A is worth 20 marks
- Section B is worth 30 marks.

As you can see, section A is worth 10 marks less than section B and it is also structured differently from the other two sections, and in this chapter we will offer you some thoughts about how to approach each of the sections of the unit with this mark breakdown in mind. When we look at the structure of Unit 4 in more detail, you will get a better idea of how it all slots together.

Section A is about you as director preparing a rehearsal for your company around a specific extract from the chosen text that will be set by the Examination Board.

Section B is about you as director responding to a focus question on how you might bring a proposed production of the chosen text to life for an audience.

Section C is about you responding to a play from a specified time period in performance, and is worth 30 marks.

You will have seen at least one performance as part of the course so far and there will have been areas of that performance that will have had an impact on you and may give you ideas as you now look at Unit 4. Your own experience of exploring, performing and devising will also have an influence on your understanding of the way drama works in performance. For this section, you will go to see another play in performance, the specific time period for that play dictated by the choice of text your teacher makes for section A and section B. An examiner will assess your responses to the questions in all three sections and your work will be marked against a set of published criteria.

THE FOCUS OF UNIT 4

Unit 4 brings together the thinking you have developed over the course of this A level and gives you an opportunity to demonstrate, through the written examination, your understanding of the way theatre works.

Although it is necessary for the examination to take the form of a written paper, a great deal of your preparation for this examination will be practical and will involve your demonstrating skills you have gained throughout the course.

The specification is available in electronic form online at www.edexcel.org.uk. You may wish to look up all the assessment criteria yourself as you progress through the A2 year. Your teacher will have access to this information and any updates as they occur, and may download and print this information for you or display it at regular intervals during the preparation process.

THE IMPORTANCE OF THE UNIT

The whole unit is worth 30 per cent of your A level marks and the examiner who marks your responses will be looking for you to offer confident and considered responses in order to enable you to access the marks. Your teacher will guide, direct and teach you with the assessment criteria in mind.

This unit covers a lot of ground, but what it also effectively does is to build on your experience of the AS year and Unit 3, and you should always have in your mind the skills you are developing to help your understanding of how drama works across the whole of this specification, leading to the requirements of Unit 4.

DECISIONS YOU NEED TO MAKE FOR UNIT 4

Unit 4 is really about the director, and this is your opportunity to demonstrate your understanding of how a director will influence the process and performance of the chosen text. Although this may seem very straightforward, there are decisions you have to make in order for you to be able to access the marks for this unit and to reach your full potential. As director, you will need to decide on approaches to rehearsals and performance concepts that you will be able to explore in order to prepare you for the examination. A lot of what you will do will be practical but, because the unit is a written examination that is worth 30 per cent of the marks for your A level, it is really important that you have an opportunity to develop your skills in relation to the questions the Examination Board will set.

Your teacher will have an understanding of the criteria, but it is important for you to note how the marks are broken down. This is something that we will be going through with you in this chapter. You will need to consider the mark structure and criteria carefully with your teacher in order to ensure that you are able to access the full range of marks in your written responses in the examination.

The 'given' of the examination is that for section A and section B *you* are the director, and there is no negotiation here. Whatever has gone before for you on this course, you will now need to be able to demonstrate an understanding of how a director will work with a company to bring a text to life, and the examiner will be marking your work on this basis. You may feel that you are more designer or performer than director but this must not come across in your response. It is important as you look at this section of the book that you have *director* at the forefront of your mind.

The Examiner says:

This unit is your opportunity to demonstrate your understanding of the way a director might work with his or her company in order to bring a text to life. You need to draw on all of your experiences of being directed in Unit 2 and of creating your Unit 3 performance. It is important that you have a clear idea of the work of the director and you are able to communicate this in your writing in section A and B particularly.

In Section C we will be looking for your understanding of how you were engaged by the performance you have seen in relation

to its historical context – what has the director done to bring it to life for you?

You are responding to three questions in 150 minutes and you will have your annotated copy of the script in front of you and your notes on the play you have seen in performance. These two supporting documents are there to guide your thinking in responding to the questions; they are not, in themselves, the answers to the questions.

Extension Activity

Review of the overview

Read this overview of Unit 4 again and summarise its main points on a postcard. Keep the postcard somewhere safe – or display it with others in the drama space – as a reminder of the focus of Unit 4.

UNIT 4: SOME GUIDANCE FOR THOSE WHO MAY STRUGGLE WITH WRITTEN EXAMINATIONS

It is unlikely that you will have reached this stage in your A level course without hearing of:

quality of written communication.

Your teacher will certainly be aware of this and may even have spoken to the group about what it means in relation to the individual units. There is a percentage of students who relish the opportunity to express thoughts, feelings and ideas on paper and who look forward to the written elements of all their subjects. There are others, of course, who feel that they are going to struggle with this particular demand. In this section, we are going to focus on written communication specifically in relation to Unit 4 but you may feel that the information given here may be useful in other aspects of your course – Unit 3 SWED, for example, or, indeed your other subjects. Quality of written communication is as much about your use of the English language as it is about your demonstration of an understanding of specific Drama and Theatre Studies words and phrases. Ideally, there should be a balance here in that you are demonstrating the one through the application of the other and it is this balance that is often disrupted in examination conditions, and you feel that all you are able to do is write down everything you know and hope that it makes some kind of sense to the examiner.

While there can never be any guarantees in anything we offer in this book, there are steps you can take in order to prepare yourself for written examinations.

Gather your thoughts

In your notebook, it might be worth gathering your thoughts at regular intervals in order to look for gaps in knowledge, information or understanding. If you are like a lot of students you will be very good at making notes and recording information during workshop sessions, but you are probably less conscientious when it comes to reviewing that information in order to establish how much of it you have actually understood. It is one part of the task to take notes and, if you have been doing this regularly since the start of the AS year, you should have quite a lot of information by now. The second part of the task is to review this information and see how much of it has actually made sense to you.

Go through your notebook(s) and highlight words, phrases, names, terms and expressions that you feel are important and write a separate list of these at the back of your book or create a word file for them. By isolating these elements of your notes you are effectively creating your own glossary of the course to date to support anything that you may write in the Unit 4 examination. Not everything will be relevent but you will be surprised at how much there is that will be.

Once you have completed your list, put it in alphabetical order and go through it in a methodical way, writing a sentence against each entry on your list to show that you have an understanding of what it means. It is important that you do this even for those entries that you feel are really obvious. It is also important that you write in sentences. The purpose of this activity is twofold. First, you are creating a glossary that is personal to you and your course to date, and second, you are identifying in some detail entries in your glossary that you are comfortable with in terms of being able to define meaning, along with entries that you may feel less confident about. It is good to share your glossary with somebody else in your group but it is important that your glossary is your own, created by you, using language that you are comfortable with and sentence structures that reflect your overall style of writing. There is a discipline to this but once you have created your glossary you can then keep on adding to it and reviewing it at regular intervals to make sure that your understanding of your entries is still sharp and focused. Use the sharing of your entries to fine-tune your information and to make sure that your understanding is what it should be. We are not talking about complex or complicated sentence structures here, but what we are looking for is for you to be able to write succinctly and accurately in order to demonstrate to your examiner that you have a confident grasp and understanding of the language of drama. This confidence may be evident in discussion and you will have earned marks for this in Unit 1 and Unit 3, for example, but Unit 4 is about the quality of your written communication, and you must be able to concentrate on the content, not the structure of your answers.

Extension Activity

Exploring the glossary and structuring sentences

Choose three entries either from your own glossary or from the one at the back of this book, and compile a sentence for each of the words that you think reflects your understanding without using any of the words in the entry in your sentence. Share your three words with a partner and ask for the word or phrase that your sentence is defining. If your partner struggles with this, you may need to go back to your sentence and review the definition to make it clear.

This activity can be repeated at regular intervals leading up to the Unit 4 examination and will need eventually to include specific words relating to the chosen text and theatrical time periods.

There are other ways that you might gather your thoughts to prepare for Unit 4 but what ever method you use the key to it all is:

you must write things down.

Discussion is great, but the examination is not about discussion. Good discussion in a group is an exchange of ideas and views through which the participants all contribute to the shaping of the whole. In a written task, you need to be able to offer all of the elements on your own and, however much you may feel that you have contributed to a discussion, it may be that your input was not always pertinent or relevent. In Unit 4, your contribution must be pertinent and relevent and expressed effectively in order to make the point for your examiner.

Order your thoughts

Once your thoughts are gathered, you must be able to order them so you know which are relevent and why to support your responses to specific questions. You may look at your glossary and divide the information under the following headings:

- Acting techniques
- Elements of the theatre
- Historical information
- Performance terms and expressions
- Practitioners
- Rehearsal techniques
- The role of the director.

You may find that there is some overlap and there may be some words and phrases that you want to expand into headings in their own right (e.g. total theatre). Part of the process of ordering your thoughts is to make a decision as to the structure and content of your glossary. The above headings are there just to guide you. If you have created an electronic list, then it is very straightforward to cut and paste it into the order you are looking for. If you have handwritten it, then you will need to spend a little more time on the headings and the list and writing out the information again. In many ways this is a more productive exercise for you, particularly if you are trying to familiarise yourself with this created glossary and to gain confidence in expressing your thoughts on paper. A copy-and-paste exercise is useful, but a writing-and-ordering exercise is much more so.

You know that Unit 4 is divided into the three sections, each of which has a different emphasis attached to it. Once you have ordered your thoughts and created your lists under the headings that you think are most appropriate, you need to review the information again and look towards which section in the examination each piece of information will be most useful for. Again, there will be some overlap, and that is inevitable, but using a different coloured pen or font, go through your list and put either A, B or C next to each entry.

Your thoughts are now in order but your lists may not be complete as yet, so do not be afraid to add more information as you go through the preparation process for Unit 4. There has been very little targeting yet, apart from letters to indicate which section of the examination paper you think each entry might support, so there is nothing to lose by adding more entries to your list.

PAUSE FOR THOUGHT

How useful is all this?

Review where you are with this. You can make as many lists as you like but they are only useful if you actually take the information and apply it to your preparation. There needs to be a consistency in your approach to this exercise, and a good way of gauging this is to look back over your entries in your glossary and see if you have written in the same detail on those entries that you made most recently, compared to those that you made at the start of the process.

You may feel that this exercise is not useful at all and you just want to get on with writing responses to practice questions rather than making lists and giving definitions of words and phrases. This exercise is designed to give you the thinking behind your responses to the questions in the examination to boost your confidence before you go into the examination room, knowing that you have put some time in for effective preparation.

Focus your thoughts

Consider the following question: *As a director, outline and justify your approach to the production of your chosen text for a specific audience of your choice.*

This may be a typical section B question and you will need to look at the demands it makes on you in relation to the information you have to take in to the examination with you. Remember, you are allowed to take in your annotated copy of the chosen text and your theatre evaluation notes of up to 1,000 words to support your response to section C. There is only so much information that you can absorb in a relatively short period of time in an examination room, so it is probably not wise to take in too much within your annotated text, for the simple reason that you will not have time to access it in the examination and answer the questions as well. To focus your thoughts you need to have an understanding of the kinds of questions that are likely to appear and a practised approach to structuring your response. You know that you are director in sections A and B and you know that you are an informed member of an audience for section C. With this information you know that you need a vocabulary to support **director** and a vocabulary to support **audience**, with some overlap between the two as and when appropriate.

We have a chapter in this section where we look at deconstructing the questions, but it is important that you understand what the question is asking of you. It is very easy to get caught up in the excitement of the moment and nerves will kick in, leading you to answer the question that you think has been set, rather than the one that is actually in front of you. This is less likely to be the case if you have taken a methodical approach to preparing for the written demands of the unit. This is not about the preparation for the questions your teacher will do with you; this is about you as an individual taking the time to support your work above and beyond what you may be doing in the studio.

The sample question opposite draws on as many aspects of your chosen text in performance as you may want to detail but, wrapped up in this is the real danger of losing focus in your response by just telling your examiner everything you can in 50 minutes but not addressing the question. In the deconstructing section we look at some specific examples of what might be included in each paragraph, but in this chapter you need to be clear that you understand the focus of the question and the information you need to include in order to access the marks. If you go back to your lists, you need to decide how these will help you to access the question. Will the work of a practitioner lead your response for your specific audience or do you feel that your approach to a particular theme or issue from the text will be more appropriate? This particular sample question has a focus on a specific audience and you must address this in your question, but otherwise the content of the response is entirely up to you. The answer you give is generic, the mark scheme is specific, so beware!

Starters and closers

In order to make sure you are able to offer specific information in your answers, you need to be able to tune into your response with a strong opening paragraph. Your concluding paragraph should also bring your thoughts together in order to give your examiner a summary to your answer in relation to the specifics of the question. It is probably a good idea to practise your opening and concluding paragraphs to a variety of questions on a regular basis, particularly for section B and section C, but the same principle could also apply to section A.

The process thus far is:

- Gather your thoughts
- Order your thoughts
- Focus your thoughts
- Explore starters and closers.

There is a progression through these steps from gathering information to the application of ideas in relation to specific questions. You need to have the information in place before you start to prepare to answer the questions.

Extension Activity

Opening paragraphs

Write the opening paragraphs for the following three questions:

- As a director, outline and justify your approach to the production of your chosen text for a specific audience of your choice.
- As a director, outline and justify your approach to one design element in the production of your chosen text.
- As a director, outline and justify your approach to the staging of your chosen text in space with which you are familiar.

Note the similarities in the questions but also note the differences and what the main consideration is in each one in seeking your specific response to it. Share your responses with a friend and look for whether or not you have engaged with the question and have set the scene for what is to come.

Consider the following as a possible opening paragraph to the question we posed earlier in the chapter (p. 71).

WORKED EXAMPLE

> I am going to justify my approach to Woyzeck with a specific audience in mind. In my audience I would like to have Year 12 drama students from the local schools and colleges in order to let them know what is expected from this unit but also to give them some ideas about the practitioner Artaud who has heavily influenced my approach. My production will be staged in our drama studio, in traverse with a minimal use of costume, set and other design elements, but what I intend to use will have real impact on the audience.

What does this tell you about the proposed production in relation to the question, and does it successfully set out for the examiner what is to follow? When you have read it, you may want to rewrite it in your own words and in a style you think will set out your ideas for the examiner for your chosen text if it is not *Woyzeck*.

Your opening paragraph should hit the ground running and help you to gather your thoughts together too with the question and concept in mind. The more you can practise opening paragraphs the more likely it is that you will be able to structure an effective one on the day that will lead your examiner into your answer.

The same is true of closing paragraphs that should draw your thoughts together and leave the examiner with an impression of a rounded and measured response to the question. Elements of the closing paragraph can be essentially the same as those of the opening paragraph.

Look at the following example in relation to the opening paragraph overleaf.

WORKED EXAMPLE

> As you can see, I have justified my approach to Woyzeck with a specific audience in mind. For my audience of Year 12 drama students from the local schools and colleges I have set out an approach to the play that lets them know what is expected from this unit but also gives them some ideas about the practitioner Artaud who has heavily influenced my approach. My production as staged in our drama studio, in traverse with a minimal use of costume, set and other design elements, can be justified to have real impact on the audience.

As a concluding paragraph, this serves to draw the threads of the ideas together and it lets the examiner know that the ideas that are presented on the page are now complete.

THE THREE TEXTS IN CONTEXT

We have included here some general background information on the time periods from which the three texts for Unit 4 have been drawn. It is a potted history, clearly having huge gaps in the historical contexts, but it should give you a flavour of the time periods and, in the case of *Woyzeck*, for example, an indication of how out of step the play was when it was written.

Lysistrata by Aristophanes in context

Not only did the Greeks produce many lasting comedies, they also opened the door for many Roman, Elizabethan and modern comedies. The historical development of comedy was not as well recorded as that of tragedy in Greek theatre. Aristotle comments in *The Poetics* that before his own time comedy was considered trivial and common – though, when it was finally recognised as an art form, the work of Aristophanes within the style of Old Comedy became instantly recognisable.

Figure III.1
Claire Higgins in *Hecuba* by Euripides at the Donmar Warehouse in 2009

It appears that Greek comedy comprised two periods of development. These fell into the categories of Old Comedy represented by Cratinus and Aristophanes; and New Comedy, whose main exponent appears to have been Menander. Aristophanes' theatrical works were presented at the Athenian festivals and he and Cratinus used three actors, a chorus that sung, danced, and sometimes participated in the dialogue. The Chorus's address to the audience reveals the author's opinion. In these speeches, he ridicules the Gods, Athenian institutions, and popular and powerful individuals, including Aeschylus, Sophocles and Euripides. Given the cultivated and scholarly culture of its ruling elite, the city of Athens invited satire. Aristophanes assumed the task with zeal, aiming his satirical jibes at those who thought themselves to be above the crowd and, indeed, those who were literally above the crowd – the Gods!

The Athenian audiences of the day were well versed in their highbrow culture and must have enjoyed the in-jokes that were a staple of the style of Old Comedy immensely. Aristophanes' other targets included the great tragic playwrights Aeschylus and Euripides, whom Aristophanes portrayed variously as a 'windbag' and 'corrupter of youth' with his heretical ideas. Aeschylus died in 456 BC (some ten years or so before Aristophanes was born) but Euripides was a near-contemporary of Aristophanes, with his death in the same year as Sophocles in 406 BC heralding the beginning of the end for the golden age of Athenian Theatre.

New Comedy

History tells us that, for the most part, comedy developed along similar lines as tragedy, becoming more aimed at the common people and less concerned with its religious origins. By 317 BC, around 80 years after the death of Aristophanes, a new form had evolved that resembled what we would probably liken to farce today. The use of overt satire, topicality and the pointed ridiculing of celebrated personalities of the day to be found in Aristophanes' style were replaced by the use of mistaken identities, ironic situations, ordinary (everyday) characters and wit. This period is called New Comedy, and its two main practitioners were Menander and Phlyates. Menander is the more significant of the two. Most of his plays are now lost, but parts found their way into plays by the Roman playwrights Plautus and Terence (whom Julius Caesar called 'a half-Menander'). From these works they were incorporated into Shakespeare's *Comedy of Errors*, Stephen Sondheim's *A Funny Thing Happened on the Way to the Forum*, even the writings of St Paul: 'Bad messages belie good manners'. In 1905 a manuscript was discovered in Cairo that contained pieces of five Menander plays, and in 1957 a complete play, *Diskolos* (*The Grouch*, 317 BC), was unearthed in Egypt. Menander's main contribution was to create a comedy model that greatly influenced later comedy, right up to the present day. Unlike Aristophanes, his characters were not celebrities or Gods but ordinary people. The chorus in Menander's plays resembled a modern chorus – singers and dancers who provided entertainment between acts, with Menander sometimes portraying them as drunken audience members. His characters were classic comedy archetypes, such as the curmudgeonly old man in *The Grouch*, who would become staples of comedy. Most of all, the style of comedy that Menander created, with its emphasis on mistaken identity, romance and situational humour, became the model for subsequent comedy, from the Romans to Shakespeare to the West End and Broadway.

The beginning of the end

By the time of Sophocles' death in 406 BC, 128 years after Thespis' victory in the first Athenian drama competition, the golden era of Greek drama was waning. Athens, whose freethinking culture had nurtured the infant theatre of the Western world, would be overrun in 404 BC by the Spartans. It would later be torn apart by constant warring with other city states, eventually falling under the dominion of Alexander the Great and his Macedonian armies.

Theatre survived, with, for example, Aristophanes continuing to write almost up to his death in 385 BC, but it would not return to the same creative heights and influence until Elizabethan England and the work of specifically Marlowe and Shakespeare two millennia later.

Stages and styles of presentation

According to tradition, the first tragedian, Thespis, performed his plays on wagons with which he travelled, and seats were set up for performances in the agora or marketplace of Athens. By the end of the sixth century BC, however, a permanent theatron, or 'watching place', was set up in the precinct of Dionysus on the southern slope of the Athenian Acropolis. Since at first any construction above ground was made of wood, and since the theatre was later rebuilt many times, facts about the surviving remains of this earliest Theatre of Dionysus are extremely scanty. Most representations of this theatre are therefore based on the evidence from other Greek theatres and on the evidence of the plays performed there. The only features which necessarily existed in the early fifth century are wooden seats for spectators on the hillside, and a level earth-floored orchestra, or 'dancing area' in the centre. The orchestra is usually believed to have been circular, with, for example, the orchestra at Epidaurus having a diameter of just over 20 metres.

Most of the surviving plays also appear to make use of a building, the skene or scene building. This was used as a changing room for actors and probably as a device to channel sound towards the audience, but it also served to represent the palace or house in front of which most plays are set. At first, it must have been a temporary building re-erected each year (skene means merely 'tent' or 'hut'). The number of doors in its façade is disputed, with most tragedies requiring only one, but it is more likely that there were three entrances, with clearly defined functions attached to each. Actors and chorus could enter by paths, called parodoi or eisodoi, to the right and left of the skene. Chiefly they made these entrances on horse-drawn chariots. The roof of the building could be used as an acting area for watchmen, gods and others. There is some suggestion in two texts of the period that screens with architectural images were used, not 'sets' for specific plays, but permanent fixtures. It is conceivable, too, that there may have been an underground passage, allowing ghosts to appear from below. The existence of a stage (logeion) in front of the skene, raising the actors above the orchestra where the chorus performed, is often disputed. The evidence for this is sparse, but it is probable that this stage existed, although it will not have been so high as to prevent easy interaction between actors and chorus. Other features of the orchestra were a central altar with several images of gods which could be referenced in the plays when required.

Doctor Faustus by Christopher Marlowe in context

Elizabethan theatre and the name of William Shakespeare are inextricably bound together, yet there were others writing plays at the same time as the bard of Avon. One of the most successful, and therefore most remembered, was Christopher Marlowe, who many contemporaries considered to be Shakespeare's superior. Marlowe's career, however, was cut short at a comparatively young age when he died in a tavern fight in Deptford, the victim of a knife in the eye. There are many theories about what happened and why Marlowe should have been in this particular tavern at this time but, suffice it to say, the full facts of the incident will probably never now be known.

Christopher Marlowe, the first master of blank verse, was born in 1564, and lived for only 29 intriguing years before his life was cut short. He was the son of a shoemaker, and he attended Cambridge University on a scholarship from the Archbishop of Canterbury, where he earned a Bachelor's degree. The scholarship had been given with the understanding that Marlowe would become a minister, but Marlowe seems to have had other ideas. Cambridge awarded him a MA, but only after the Queen's Privy Council spoke up on his behalf, possibly, it has been suggested, as part of his compensation for espionage conducted on the Continent. He then left Cambridge to write plays for the emerging theatres of London. Marlowe became a member of the School of Night, along with Sir Walter Raleigh and the mathematician John Dee, and he was also suspected of homosexuality and atheism, and was actually picked up and questioned about his religious beliefs just days before his death in the tavern brawl – which itself has led to speculation about assassination – in 1593. This event did nothing to dispel the commonly held opinion that theatre had an unsavory reputation. London authorities refused to allow plays within the city, so theatres opened across the Thames in Southwark, outside the authority of the city administration. The first proper theatre as we know it was the Theatre, built at Shoreditch in 1576. Before this time plays were performed in the courtyards of inns, or sometimes in the houses of noblemen. A noble had to be careful about which play he allowed to be performed within his home, however. Anything that was controversial or political was likely to lead to questioning by representatives of the Crown.

After the Theatre, further open-air playhouses opened in the London area, including the Rose (1587) and the Hope (1613). The most famous playhouse was the Globe (1599), built by the company in which Shakespeare had a stake, opened just six years after the death of Marlowe. The Globe was only in use until 1613, when a cannon fired during a performance of *Henry VIII* caused the roof to catch fire and the building burned to the ground. The site of the theatre was rediscovered in the twentieth century and a reconstruction was built as close to the spot as possible in a project driven by the actor Sam Wanamaker, with the reconstructed building opening in 1997.

Figure III.2
Zoe Wannamaker in Shakespeare's *Much Ado About Nothing* at the National Theatre in 2008

These theatres could hold several thousand people, most standing in the open pit in front of the stage, though rich nobles could watch the play from a chair set to the side of the stage itself. Theatre performances were held in the afternoons, because, of course, there was no artificial lighting. Women attended plays, though prosperous women would often wear masks to disguise their identity. In the theatre of the time no women performed in the plays; female roles were generally performed by young men.

Woyzeck by Georg Buchner in context

Although written in 1836, this play was not performed until 1913 and it therefore spans nearly 80 years of theatrical development and is often regarded as a forerunner of naturalism and expressionism. Buchner died of typhus before his twenty-fourth birthday, leaving three plays, all of which remained unperformed until the turn of the twentieth century. The play itself was therefore in existence, gathering dust and unperformed, against a backdrop of theatrical developments, some of which are briefly included here. In the late eighteenth and early nineteenth centuries, the outstanding movement in the dramatic field was that of romanticism as against the classicism of most earlier European drama. In France, the nineteenth century added the names of Victor Hugo, Eugène Scribe, Émile Augier, Alexander Dumas the younger and Victorien Sardou to its list of theatrical entrepreneurs.

In England a literary or 'closet' drama, almost entirely unsuited to stage production due to its almost total reliance on word play, sprang up. It listed among its contributors such names as Wordsworth, Coleridge, Byron, Shelley, Swinburne, Browning and Tennyson. It was not until the latter part of the century that the English stage again showed signs of life with the advent of Henry Arthur Jones, Sir Arthur Wing Pinero and Oscar Wilde.

The latter part of this century, too, saw the beginning of the independent theatre movement that was to be the forerunner of the Little Theatre movement that spread far and wide during the twentieth century. It was in such theatres as the *Théâtre Libre* of Paris, *Die Freie Bühne* of Berlin, the *Independent Theatre* of London and *Miss Horniman's Theatre* in Manchester that Ibsen, Strindberg, Björnson, Yeats, Shaw, Hauptmann and Synge were first given a hearing.

Around the same time in Germany there appeared two dramatists who would go on to win international fame: Hauptmann and Sudermann. In France, Brieux became the herald of a realistic, not to say clinical drama. Belgium produced Maeterlinck. But the most notable event of the late nineteenth century was probably the production in Paris of Edmond Rostand's *Cyrano de Bergerac*.

In Spain José Echegaray, author of *The World and His Wife*; José Benavente, whose *Passion Flower* and *Bonds of Interest* were offered on the American stage; and the brothers Sierra, whose *Cradle Song* achieved international fame, are a connecting link between the nineteenth and twentieth centuries, as are Shaw, Galsworthy and Barrie in England, and Lady Augusta Gregory and W. B. Yeats in Ireland.

If we go back to the start of the nineteenth century, we can see that in the early 1800s theatre attendance lessened, due partly to economic decline and poor standards of acting and production. Patronage by the middle classes also fell as a result of theatre's increasingly bad reputation and raucous nature, a result of opening the doors to those who had previously been largely ignored by the theatre's 'élite' but who were to provide a much-needed lifeline to struggling theatre, even if the performances themselves took a different turn towards melodrama.

The Industrial Revolution saw many people from the country migrate to the expanding industrial towns. This resulted in the decline of rural theatres, although some touring companies around the country continued to operate, but mainly from barn fit-ups. In the more populated urban centres, however, there was a significant increase in theatre building.

In 1843, the Theatres Act legislated against the consumption of alcohol in the auditorium. This led to the closure of many small saloon theatres, which relied upon alcohol sales to stay in business. Yet the same legislation enabled magistrates to grant public houses licences to offer a variety of entertainment, and which led to the creation of a new form of popular theatrical entertainment known as music-hall. Very soon, concert or supper rooms were built on to public houses which could sell alcohol and serve meals during their musical productions. These were usually well-lit rooms with a flat floor and a simple open platform stage with little or no scenery. The audience would sit on benches or at tables in front of the stage, or on balconies against one or more of the walls. They could come and go freely during the evening and were not restricted to performance times.

Eventually a specific type of theatre building was developed to cater for this new form of entertainment, called a music-hall. These had fewer tables in front of the stage, using the space for benched seating to accommodate more people. Hundreds were built in working-class areas as money-making concerns, catering for the needs of the local clientele. Like theatres, successful music-halls were so popular that they were demolished and replaced by larger halls to accommodate even more customers.

New theatres incorporated boxes, in which only a few people sat. Although these were close to the stage, they did not have the best views. But, just like those in Shakespeare's theatre seated at the edge of the stage, they allowed the rich to sit apart from the rest of the audience in a prominent position, enabling them to be seen and admired in all their finery and jewellery. In some theatres the boxes were large enough to be used as a social space, with curtains that could be closed so that the occupants could enjoy supper or drinks.

By the mid-nineteenth century, theatre building in Great Britain was becoming a specialist architectural discipline, led by architects such as J. T. Robinson and C. J. Phipps. They were tasked with building even bigger theatres, with grander front-of-house arrangements and more luxurious social areas. Often, older theatres, like the music-halls mentioned overleaf, were demolished and rebuilt to accommodate larger audiences. In the auditoriums, rectangular galleries began to be replaced by horseshoe-shaped balconies that enveloped the stage and provided better viewing. The intention was to bring respectability to theatre-going and to make it more socially acceptable for the middle classes once more. To achieve this, different classes were segregated:

- financially by the cost of the tickets
- physically by the requirement to use separate entrances and exits and circulation routes.

The rich entered via illuminated entrances with grand staircases and rich carpets, while the cheaper seats were accessed via smaller side or rear entrances, with less grand staircases and public areas. At the same time, the benched pit in front of the stage was replaced by more comfortable seats and carpeted aisles for the rich. The cheaper seats were now restricted to the rear stalls behind a wooden barrier, known as the 'pit', and the balcony or gallery. Although theatre was enjoyed by much of the population, it was not always accessible throughout Britain. In rural areas of Wales, for example, the portable theatre was popular. These theatres toured the country and could be dismantled and moved easily. They were well supported in the small towns and villages which could not sustain permanent theatrical venues, and survived until World War I.

Despite strong competition from other theatre forms, melodrama was the primary form of theatre during the nineteenth century, despite other influences, becoming the most popular by 1840. Melodrama is still with us today. Very simply, the evolution of melodrama may be traced as follows:

- In the early 1800s, most were romantic, exotic or supernatural.
- In the 1820s, they became more familiar in settings and characters.
- In the 1830s, they became more elevated: 'gentlemanly' melodrama.

Alongside the developments in melodrama, there was increased interest in historical accuracy and an interest in the unusual or exotic, leading to, for example, authentic folk dances and costumes and picturesque settings became more common on stage. Charles Kemble's production of Shakespeare's *King John* in London in 1823 was the first to claim complete historical accuracy. By 1850, it appeared that it was important everywhere.

Realism of spectacle led to the elimination of the staples of the scenic designer, the wing and drop sets, and the development of the 'box set', with three walls and perhaps a ceiling to represent interiors. This interest in 'realism' also led to the levelling of the stage floor, stagehands moving scenery manually (though grooves or chariot-and-pole systems were still used), revolving stages, elevators, rolling platforms, groundrows (cutaway flats), closed front curtains, acting upstage of the proscenium line (rather than on the apron), and the more general acceptance of the fourth wall convention. With the use of electric lighting, which illuminated the set much more efficiently, there was an increased need for greater scenic realism, but the plays themselves were still romantic and melodramatic. The movement of Realism would shake things up a bit.

box set
A set that as far as possible represents the space in which the action takes place, usually referring to a room in a house, and so-called as it creates a 'box' into which the actors enter and exit through realistic doors and are confined in the space, usually not breaking the fourth wall.

12 The demands of section A

With this background information in mind, you may want to consider an approach to section A for the chosen text that will demonstrate your understanding of theatre of the time as detailed here and in your further background research. The examiner is looking for you to be creative and imaginative – but also realistic in an approach to the chosen text in section A. There should be a confidence in the response which leads the examiner into your thoughts in relation to both the text and a considered approach to it in relation to the question that has been asked. The questions in section A and B are about rehearsal and performance but the responses will indicate an understanding of the text and its historical context that enables you to bring it to life for company and audience through rehearsal and performance.

APPROACHING SECTION A

It is important to remember as you approach this unit that there are no right or wrong answers to these questions, as long as it is clear in your response to section A and section B that you are remaining true to the playwright's original intentions and demonstrating an understanding of its historical context as far as we know it. The examiner is looking for an imaginative but practical response to the question that demonstrates an understanding of creating theatre that may have been gained through other aspects of the course. This is your opportunity in the A2 year to engage with an examiner who is keen to see what you have understood about the way performance may be shaped by a director in order to influence audience reaction and understanding.

FOCUS

The focus of section A is rehearsal and the question is divided into three parts, with each part looking for a response to a given extract from the text.

The extract will be from a significant moment in the text and will look to you to be able to recognise appropriate rehearsal techniques and to apply them to the demands of rehearsing the extract in relation to the questions. This focus question is looking for a demonstration of understanding of the director working with the company, with the extract being the focal point of the response.

Extension Activity

The role of the director

- In pairs, draw up a job description of the ideal director and, based on this, write down three questions you would ask of candidates at interview for the job of directing a production of your chosen text.
- Use your job description and your three questions for the basis of a class discussion on the role of director in the theatre and in specific relation to the chosen text.

REHEARSAL TECHNIQUES

There is no preconceived idea in the unit as to what is an appropriate rehearsal technique or strategy, but you will need to justify decisions in relation to an understanding of the chosen text and demonstrate in the response how the approach will help develop rehearsal leading to performance. There may be a heavy reliance on practitioners in this section, with students referring back to other units and the influence of practitioners on their work.

While there is every intention that you should be encouraged to be making connections there must also be an awareness that not all practitioners may be suitable for providing explorative strategies or production concepts for all texts. You bring ideas to focus in section A that will indicate very clearly your understanding of an appropriate approach to rehearsal in relation to the given extract and the text as a whole.

It may well be that you have used rehearsal strategies that have no specific practitioner atttached to them. These may arise from rehearsal activities and have influence rooted in the work of specific practitioners but which are less rigid than recognisable techniques we would normally associate with that practitioner's work. Your teacher may have a particular strategy for exploring non-verbal communication, for example, that you pick up on and develop in your own work which in turn could be used in response to a question on *Woyzeck*. This is also acceptable but such techniques may need more of an explanation within an answer than 'marking the moment', for example. Not everything you do might have a name attached to it, but that does not make it any less valid in relation to strategies you may employ as a director rehearsing with a company to explore an extract from the chosen text.

REHEARSAL STRATEGIES

You need to explore the chosen text from the viewpoint of a director working with a company preparing the script for performance. In this section of the exam paper you will be asked to offer your strategies for rehearsing an extract from the play with your company. The question is about rehearsal and it is looking for you to have an understanding of the purpose and structure of rehearsal in order to access the higher level marks that are available here. The more focused your response in relation to the extract and the appropriate use of rehearsal techniques and strategies, the more likely it will be that you will be able to access the marks. This question is not just about rehearsal, but it is about rehearsing the extract, and you need to recognise the difference here. If you are not prepared sufficiently for the question, the temptation will be just to write as much as you can about rehearsal and hope that some of the points you are making will earn you some marks. This is not a recommended strategy for this level of study. In order to be able to focus your responses, you need to have practically explored the text in the A2 year and used your understanding of the play to choose rehearsal techniques that are appropriate to the play and your proposed interpretation.

Draw on your experiences of exploring and rehearsing from the AS year. You will have been involved in a great deal of practical work during the preparation for Unit 2 and in exploring the two texts for Unit 1. All of this work will be useful in helping you to prepare for Unit 4, and it is good practice to recognise the connections and to refer back to your notes from the AS year to remind yourself of strategies that worked then and which may work for you in considering Unit 4.

The Examiner says:

Make the connections and earn the marks

If you are able to make the connections across the experiences you have had on this course, you are more likely to be able to access the top band of marks in all four units. There are particular challenges in this unit compared to the others, but do not forget the written work you have produced so far and how that was shaped by the structures given in the specification. All of that experience of preparing focused and targeted written responses should have helped to prepare you for the demands of the written examination. You have written about drama and written about it successfully; otherwise you would not be here now. There is no doubt that a large number of students have particular difficulty in accessing marks in written examinations for drama and theatre studies. If you feel that you may be one of these students, you will need to think about how you are going to access the questions as soon as you possibly can in the A2 year and to start to prepare timed responses. It is not enough to know the text in this unit; you will need to be able to convince an examiner that you have valid strategies in mind for rehearsal and performance and, more importantly, that you are able to apply your ideas to the question that you have been asked. The Exam Board has published a sample examination paper and mark scheme that your teacher should have access to and, after 2010, there will be papers from previous years available to give you an idea of the way the pattern of questions is emerging. As with all examinations, there is only a limited range of experiences that can be explored within any examination paper and there will be a generic feel to the tone and focus of the questions for Unit 4 once we have established the pattern.

Go back into your own rehearsal experience and list the rehearsal techniques or strategies that you feel helped you the most. These experiences may or may not connect you with a practitioner and strategies may or may not have a formal name or label attached to them. The important thing for you to consider when looking at preparing for this section of Unit 4 is the confidence with which you will be able to answer the questions based on your own practical experience of rehearsing for performance.

The rehearsal question that forms section A is broken down into three parts, with each part having its own mark structure. You will see that for your 20 marks you need to provide answers that will earn you up to four, six and ten marks each. All three parts of the question relate to the extract and you need to try to keep your response focused on the extract and not be too general about the play as a whole. We will have more to say about this later in the chapter, but, for the moment, it is worth looking at some rehearsal strategies and how these relate to the kind of questions that might be set in this section.

Before you start looking at rehearsal strategies in detail you need to have an understanding of the play and its historical context. The brief summary at the start of this chapter will give you some idea, but it is always good practice to find time to read the play in your own time and to make notes of any passages that you struggle with during this reading. If you are struggling, there is a very good chance that others in your group are struggling too. You may want to revisit some of the ideas we had in AS *Drama and Theatre Studies* on accessing scripts and approaches to preparing a script for performance. The ideas on reading for meaning and reading for understanding, for example, are as valid for this unit as they were for Unit 2. It is likely that your teacher will lead you through a series of rehearsals on extracts from the text and give you the opportunity to research its social, historical, cultural and political context.

Research as a rehearsal strategy is perfectly valid as long as it is seen as research and not downloading pages of connected information that may or may not be relevent to the task you have been set. You may want to try the following Extension Activity that is very much focused on section A of Unit 4 in preparing your script for performance.

Extension Activity

Research with a focus

There are three strands to this research which you may like to do in groups of three, with each of you taking responsibility for one of the strands.

The strands are:

- Playwright
- Play
- Context

1. Find out all that you can about the playwright. Is this play the one that he is known for or is it a relatively minor example of his work? Does the play sit comfortably with his other works or does it stand out for some reason? What does the play say about the playwright's view of life at the time of writing?
2. Find out what you can about the play itself and its production history. Was it a popular play in its time or has it grown in popularity since its original performance? What does the play tell us about theatre and performance at the time of writing? How typical is the play of what an audience would have expected at the time? Are there themes explored in the text that an audience of the day would have found challenging and how do we feel about those themes today?
3. What is the context of the play? What was going on in the rest of society when it was written? Is it a true reflection of the tastes and thoughts of the time or was it challenging to its audience in its day? How much of a reflection of the thoughts, feelings, views and opinions of the general populace of the time of writing do your think the play is?

This is one way of focusing your research on the chosen text and it may be interesting for you to present your findings, as a group, to the rest of the class who, we presume, have also been given a similar task. By repeating the same task (or variations on the same task) you may find that you will create a more complete picture of the play in its historical context which will then enable you as an individual to see more clearly where you want to go with it in order to bring your interpretation to life for your twenty-first-century audience. The three time periods chosen for this unit have been extensively explored and documented over the years and there is an enormous amount of information available to anybody tasked with carrying out research on any one of them. This is why it is important that your research is targeted and specific to the play and the playwright first, and any other material is then seen in relation to those two strands of research. You need to have sufficient information from your research to enable you to come to some educated and informed conclusions about the possible impact on the audience of the day of the play in its original performance conditions.

POSSIBLE APPROACHES TO TEXTS IN REHEARSAL

With the focus, therefore, of section A being rehearsal, you need to be confident in choosing rehearsal techniques, ideas or strategies that are appropriate to the given extract and to the demands of the individual parts of the question. The extract is at the centre of the response and everything within the response needs to connect to the extract in relation to the question and your understanding of the director working with the company. In the preparation for section A there are strategies your teacher may employ in order to ensure that you have an understanding of the purpose of rehearsal and, more importantly, are able to transmit this to an examiner through your written responses. Your teacher may lead a number of sessions with you in which you revisit some of the activities you may have been engaged in during the AS year.

If you are feeling as though you are struggling with thinking about Unit 4, or if you simply want to try to stay ahead of the game and put in some background work yourself, at an early stage in preparing for this unit it may be worth making the connections with the AS year and looking at strategies employed in exploring texts for Unit 1 and rehearsing texts for Unit 2. Your teacher will probably have the overview more clearly in place than you have so it would perhaps be a good idea for your teacher to guide you through the connections with what has gone before in relation to what is to come in Unit 4. As a participant in Units 1 and 2, however, you will have kept notes and rehearsal schedules that you need to bring out again and look at specific strategies that helped you to explore and rehearse, and to see which of these were particularly successful and why.

Extension Activity

Revisit Unit 1 and Unit 2

Go over your notes for Unit 1 and Unit 2 and look to see what strategies you employed in exploring and rehearsing. This may help you when it comes to planning for section A of Unit 4. Make a list of possible ideas to bring to a workshop session.

Your teacher will also have an idea of those students who may need more support with their written work than others, and this could influence decisions your teacher may make about structuring workshop activities around the chosen text.

There is no doubt that the more practical the preparation for the written examination is, the more it is likely that you will be able to access the marks and offer confident responses, based on your own experiences in rehearsing extracts from the text. There are no hard-and-fast rules about this but you do need to have an understanding of the purpose of rehearsal and ideas for how you might legitimately explore the chosen text as a director working with a company and to be able to offer these thoughts in a written examination.

PRACTICAL WITH THEORETICAL – MAKING THE CONNECTIONS

You need to keep at the forefront of your mind that the best way of accessing good marks for the written examination is by exploring its demands through practical drama activities. You know that section A is about rehearsal and you know that the focus is on the director in relation to a given extract. It seems logical, therefore, to make sure that you have a series of workshop activities in place that enable practical exploration in the form of rehearsals to happen and to inform. The practical activities in this series of structured workshops must connect directly into the demands of the written paper. There is little point in setting up rehearsal opportunities if there is no follow-up written work that makes the connection into the kinds of questions likely to appear in section A. The most successful workshops are those that give you the opportunity to either direct or be directed in a given extract from the play.

These workshops are successful because they potentially lead directly into the demands of the written unit, and those of you who have been actively involved are more likely than not to recall that involvement, and to use it to shape your response to a written question, particularly if this has been the construct during the preparation process.

There is a balance here between your teacher teaching those elements of the chosen text that he or she feels you need to be aware of in order to access the questions, and giving you the freedom to explore freely and practically. Ideally, one should lead into the other, and there is no doubt that there are clear teaching and learning opportunities wrapped up in your teacher's approach to preparing for Unit 4. One of the things he or she might do with you is to look back before moving you forward.

By making the connection with the other units of this specification your teacher will be guiding you towards seeing the experience you have had to date in a much broader context, enabling you to think about accessing Unit 4 through your understanding of the way drama works for director, performer and audience. All students embarking on the A2 year have developed their skills in line with the demands of the specification; not all of you will realise this unless your teacher takes you back and is able to break down the individual units and give clear examples of where the connections can be made. Look at the elements that made up the exploration of Unit 1, for example. There are clear connections to be made here in relation to approaching the chosen text for Unit 4. Look at rehearsal strategies for Unit 2, again in relation to what you might be able to do with an extract from the chosen text in Unit 4.

While there are no hard-and-fast rules about how long the extract in section A is likely to be, the prepublished material gives an idea of what might be considered reasonable for you to explore in the time allowed. Have a look at it and see it in the context of the whole script. It is not a lengthy extract but a lot goes on in it, and this is likely to be the case for future extracts used in the examination. By putting together a series of workshops based on extracts from the chosen text in sequence that enables practical exploration to take place in a structured activity, you will start to recognise potential for responses to section A based on your own use and understanding of appropriate rehearsal techniques. You are also going through the text in a practical way, without your teacher necessarily taking time to sit down to read it as a group. Your teacher may, of course, choose to read the text as a class activity and use this to fill in some of the gaps in knowledge there may be in your group around the context of the chosen text. There is more than one way your teacher can do this, depending on the make-up of the group itself.

Some of you will need more support than others at this stage. Have a look around your group; it could be that you feel you need a very structured and supportive approach in order to help you to understand exactly what is required in this section. If so, either your teacher has recognised this in you by now, or you are going to have to say something.

Should your teacher decide on a practical approach and if that approach is to be based on extracts, he or she will need to draw up a rota and allocate a director to each session in the rota, giving as many of you as possible an opportunity to direct an extract from the text in a given and structured purpose. This 'given and structured' purpose comes from your teacher and is based on his or her understanding of the kinds of questions that are likely to appear in section A. Your group may start with a block of four or five rehearsals/workshops in place initially and this information is published well in advance. There are three main reasons why your teacher does this:

- The student as director has time to prepare and to share ideas with the teacher before the session.
- The others in the group have time to read the chosen extracts in order to help them to prepare for the sessions as active participants.

- Publishing the schedule gives a formality to the activity and lends it the appropriate kudos.

WORKED EXAMPLE

Rehearsal: 3 March. Focus: pp. 3–13. Director: Jake. In planning this rehearsal, Jake, you need to consider the following:

1. Exploring the relationship between Woyzeck and Andres at the start of the extract.
2. Three appropriate rehearsal techniques you might use to highlight the different personalities of Marie and Margaret in this extract.
3. How to develop the relationship between Woyzeck and the other characters in this rehearsal with some appropriate strategies.

You will need to divide the rehearsal into three parts, each with the focus on (1), (2) or (3), and you should plan to spend ten minutes on (1), 20 minutes on (2) and 30 minutes on (3) in your workshop. You have a week to plan your rehearsal and share it with me on •••• before you lead the session.

This outline is for the first student-led workshop on the text and follows introductory work with the group on the text from their teacher. The SAMs (Sample Assessment Material) decide the focus of the workshop and this helps give a structure to an approach to the practical activities in the workshop. Jake may need support in looking at suitable approaches for his rehearsal and a reminder of other rehearsal activities he may have been involved in as part of the course to date. It is a good idea that this teacher has built some time into the programme to allow an opportunity for Jake to share his ideas before the actual workshop and for the teacher to have a look at the proposed structure. Once the template is in place it is easy to modify it to suit the way the group responds to the workshops – it is also easy for the teacher to step in and take over as necessary or to develop points in discussion that he or she feels need to be emphasised in relation to the kinds of questions that might be expected in the examination.

The teacher in this example will be able to gauge whether or not the activities Jake is proposing will lead the group towards a better understanding of this extract and its particular focus in this workshop. It may be that your teacher will lead you in a series of workshops before handing over to you and will deliberately include specific rehearsal techniques or ideas relating to specific practitioners, thus helping you to make connections with previous work. This could be really helpful and give you confidence, particularly if you are the person chosen to lead the first workshop activity with your group.

Some of you may not be as confident as others in leading workshops, so your teacher may pair you to direct an extract. The whole purpose of this kind of activity is to help you to recognise that the questions in Unit 4 are about your experience and understanding of how drama works in practice. The activity is not designed to be threatening in any way but it could be an expectation at this stage in an A level course that the vast majority of students will be confident in leading the others in workshop activities. The more practical activities you can be involved in, the more likelihood there is that you will be able to reflect on this experience.

Extension Activity

Planning a rehearsal

In relation to the equivalent extract from the text you are preparing for this section, plan a workshop activity along the lines of the one planned for Jake, breaking it down in the same way but with perhaps a different focus on various aspects of the extract.

Other workshops, again led by students, will take you through key moments in the text and, if time allows, you may even have an opportunity to go back to the start and rework your initial activities with a different focus and a different set of questions in mind. By replicating as far as possible the focus of the questions in section A, you can follow each workshop with a written task that explores the questions and how to structure responses in a given time. Your teacher may look, for example, at three extracts in a week and then set three question (a) tasks or three question (b) tasks. It is the skill of responding to the written task that you will need to develop and there is more than one way of encouraging you to do this.

The time for you to be on your own is in the examination room. Everything else that happens on the course leading up to the written examination needs to be as collective and supportive as possible, encouraging through discussion those of you who are likely to struggle in Unit 4. You might therefore follow a student-led workshop with a teacher-led discussion session where as a group you look at the possible questions from section A that could arise from the workshop and explore collectively the kinds of responses that may help you to access marks and why. By deconstructing the questions and exploring possible responses, your teacher is enabling you to gain in confidence collectively before setting you the written task for homework. The (a), (b) and (c) of the structure of the sample workshop replicates the three parts to the question in section A and gives a breakdown of an approach to responding to the set questions. Your teacher might also tackle this in reverse and follow a teacher-led workshop with a student-led discussion session, putting you on the spot to explore the relevent points you should be picking up from the workshop activity to help you to develop your written responses.

In discussion your teacher might ask:

- What did you do to explore the relationship between Woyzeck and Andres?
- What specific rehearsal techniques did you use to explore the personalities of Marie and Margaret?
- What specific strategies did you use to explore the relationship between Woyzeck and the others? How successful were you?

The responses in discussion will then lead into structuring written responses and the kinds of phrases that might be included can then be collectively explored. Compiling lists of useful words and phrases that can be dropped into written work is an ongoing activity for which the notebook and the flip chart were surely invented. Do not sit there in the hope that you will remember everything that has been said – write it down.

ASSESSMENT

Your marks are awarded against a published list of criteria. The structure of the questions and the mark scheme has been set out in a SAMs document available online from the Edexcel website. It is worth considering that this publication has been available for a while and that it will probably have shaped your teacher's approach to Unit 4 and, possibly, to Unit 3 with the written unit in mind. Ideally, Unit 4 should shape the course from the start of the AS year and opportunities should be taken regularly to reinforce the demands of the written examination by your teacher and, indeed, by us in the AS book.

From 2010 and the first series of Unit 4, actual examination papers will become available, so you will be able to see the pattern of questions and the published mark schemes which will indicate where you will be able to earn marks in your responses. The SAMs material gives a clear indication of how the questions will be structured and how the marks will be awarded.

The structure of the section A question takes you through a rehearsal for the published extract from the play. It is not about rehearsal in general, but about specific rehearsal techniques in relation to the extract and the question. The challenge for you in approaching this question lies in your ability to select and apply rehearsal techniques and ideas that are appropriate and demonstrable in response to the question that has been set.

The three parts to the question each demand a different focus on the extract and your understanding of how you, as a director, may shape a rehearsal in order to explore character in situation. It is worth pointing out again that the more practical the approach to preparing for this unit, the more opportunities there will be for you to be able to relate responses to your own practical experiences. The questions on the page may seem more daunting for those of you who cannot immediately relate a practical experience that you have been part of in a workshop to the demands of writing about an approach you might have as a director to rehearsing an extract from the play.

The rehearsal focus in this section allows for a range of responses from you and there is no intention to limit answers to a preconceived formula. Some of you may struggle with this at first, as you quite naturally want to know how to 'get it right'. As far as this question is concerned, 'getting it right' is about offering practical examples that are relevent to the extract and to rehearsal in response to the questions. Consider the following question on *Woyzeck* by Georg Buchner that is worth four marks for section A.

WORKED EXAMPLE

> Outline for your performers *two* ways they might indicate the relationship between Woyzeck and Andres at the start of this extract.

This kind of question is typical of a part (a) question in structure and tone. It is straightforward and practical and leads you into an immediate response in the available space in the answer booklet that needs to be concise and focused. The marks will come from the '*two* ways' and the reason for each of them in rehearsal. A typical response would probably be:

> In this rehearsal one way I would have my performers indicate the relationship between the two characters at the start of the extract would be by exploring their body language to indicate how mysterious Woyzeck is at this point and how Andres does not

appear to understand this as he sings and splits sticks. This will be useful for my actors as it will give each of them a different shape to explore – one open, the other (Woyzeck) closed, possibly with arms folded across his chest when he whispers at the start of the extract.

This is half of the answer, and it is important that you make the connection with rehearsal. You need to be very clear in the section that they are writing about rehearsal, not performance, so the language used in the responses must indicate this. The structure here is very simple – this is what I would do with my actors, and this is why I would do it. The second part of the response is very important, as the marks for just reporting the activity in the rehearsal cannot take it into the higher levels. You need to be aware of this.

Without the reasoning, the response will not be able to access the higher level of marks.

To earn four marks for this type of question, two clear and valid examples need to be given, each supported by reasons. The ideas should be practical and demonstrate thinking that is confident, accurate and clear, and rehearsal must be explicit in the response. If anything, considering this is only half the answer to this four-mark question, what we are offering here is too detailed and could easily be cut down.

Extension Activity

Working on responses

Take the response to *Woyzeck* part (a) and rewrite it, using two-thirds of the words but still have it say essentially the same as it says here.

It is worth having a look at the space available for the response to this question in relation to the marks. It is also worth exploring ways of structuring sentences in response to question (a) that are focused. Put very simply, this question asks you to tell the examiner:

In my rehearsal, one way is this and why; the other way is this and why.

You do not need more information than this to access the marks for this question. As long as the ideas are related to the question and the extract and are supported by reasons, you are well on the way to four marks. The marking scheme sets out clearly what you need to present in the answer in order to access those marks. There is no requirement to write two or three sides in order to access the four marks. In some cases, students who write too much for this question are not focused and do not necessarily answer the question. There is a skill that needs to be developed in answering questions as concisely as possible, particularly when you take the quality of written communication into account. There is the advantage in thinking about Unit 4 and preparing for it as early as possible in the course. You can make connections, for example, with selecting information for the elements of Unit 1 and the responses to the questions in this unit.

The second question in section A is worth six marks and looks for a little more information in the space allowed. It would be easy to say that if two points supported by reasons is the way to access four marks, then three points supported by reasons should access the six marks. While this would be logical, there is usually nothing in the question that demands or indicates this, whereas in the first question it will always stipulate *two* of something. The second question will not always stipulate three of something as it does in the SAMs material.

You need to look at the mark scheme and see where the marks are awarded for this second question.

KEY WORDS

The key words in the question on *Woyzeck* in the SAMs, for example, are:

- Three
- Appropriate
- Rehearsal techniques
- Marie and Margaret

The key word *appropriate* is, arguably, the most important, as it is asking you to differentiate between a range of rehearsal techniques and to select three that you think would help you as director to explore with your company the relationships at this point of the play. What you must avoid is the confessing approach to which students often resort under pressure – the more information I give, the more likely it is that I will be able to access the marks. Your teacher will tell you that this not to be the case and the preparation for this examination needs to give you the confidence to consider rehearsal techniques that are appropriate to the demands of the chosen text. This kind of question is typical of what may be expected in section A and preparation for the unit needs to take this into account.

The third question in section A is worth ten marks and thus is the more demanding. What has gone before in this section has led you towards this question, which tends to cover the extract in a more general way and looks to you to select examples to support rehearsal ideas. There is more space in the answer booklet for ideas to be explored and supported by specific examples.

The whole of section A therefore makes specific demands on you by asking you to demonstrate an understanding of the purpose of rehearsal in relation to focus questions and a given extract. The ideas you offer need to make sense and be appropriate to the text and the question. If there is a numerical requirement in the question, this needs to be met. There is no point in your writing about four approaches to an aspect of the rehearsal if the question specifies two. There will be no extra marks awarded for the additional information and, indeed, you may self-penalise by not being able to explore fully what the question actually asked for. These types of responses often become lists, and, while there is a need to give information in response to the question, the 'list' method should be avoided.

13 The demands of section B

Section B is about performance and the focus of the question is on your demonstrating how a director might bring the text to life for a twenty-first-century audience in relation to the given question. You are in control again here, but this section is more than about looking at rehearsal techniques to encourage your company to explore the text; it is about having a workable concept for an intended production of the chosen text that you can justify in terms of its historical, cultural, social and political context. You need to revisit the information we included earlier on the general historical contexts of the plays and to look further afield with your research in order to develop a clear picture of the play within its historical setting that will then go some way towards informing your interpretation. You cannot hope to know where you are going with this if you do not know where the play has come from.

APPROACHING SECTION B

The focus of Section B is performance. In the role of director a question will look to you to be able to recognise appropriate performance elements and to apply them to the demands of realising a production of the play in relation to the question. The focus of the question looks for a demonstration of understanding of the director working with the text and the company, with your interpretation being the focal point of the response. There is no pre-conceived idea here as to what is an appropriate interpretation, but you will need to justify decisions in relation to an understanding of the chosen text and demonstrate in the response how the approach will help develop an exciting, relevant and interesting piece of theatre for an audience. Your examiner will be looking to see how much you have understood the significance of the text and how you will approach this on behalf of your audience.

This question is not about the play, but it is about an understanding of bringing a text to life with a clear reference to its performance values. To reiterate this, therefore, you will need to be able to demonstrate an understanding of how the play might have sat within its original performance conditions in order to justify decisions made for a twenty-first-century production. Although this is a theoretical exercise you will need to be very focused in your ideas, perhaps drawing from other experiences you have had both as a performer and as a member of an audience. There is an exciting challenge for you in this section of Unit 4, and that challenge needs to be seen in the context of the theatrical experience you will be looking to define for your intended audience.

Your teacher, in guiding you, will encourage imagination and creativity in working towards this question, but we should also sound a word of caution here. The examiner is looking for a response that recognises the playwright's original intentions as far as we might be aware of them. It is not enough for you simply to present an idea based on a theatrical experience you may have had as part of the course. The concept needs to reflect a clear understanding of how to bring the chosen text to life for an audience, drawing on a wider theatrical experience but focusing on the specifics of the chosen text. You may have been excited by a *Kneehigh* production, for example, and want to take some of their performance ideas to develop within your concept. While there is nothing intrinsically wrong with this, you have to weigh up how relevant these may be to the overall impact of your production on your audience. In other words, consider this:

- Are you choosing to borrow these ideas from the *Kneehigh* production because you feel they will help communicate your concept to your audience?

  OR

- Are you choosing to use them because they are the only ideas that you have been excited by and you are going to make them fit your concept whether they are appropriate or not?

This is a difficult balance for you to make, and you will need to be guided by your teacher in order to be able to structure a concept for the text that also reflects the experience you have had at this level of study. Not everything that you will have covered may be relevant now but, by being able to reject ideas, you are much more able to focus on those that may be worth developing towards your concept.

Section B places the interpretation you have prepared into focus in response to a question that is structured in order to establish not only how effective you think the intended theatrical experience might be for an audience, but also how much you have considered the historical context of the play. It is not enough for you to have read the text, understood it and prepared a concept. Your concept, as director, needs to recognise the text's place within that theatrical canon which brings it to us in the twenty-first century, hopefully as relevant now as it was when originally performed.

There is a choice of two questions for each of the three texts in this section and you will need to weigh up the demands of each question carefully in order to be able to present responses that you hope will enable you to access the marks. When you look at sample questions you will notice that the questions across all three texts are very similar. This is deliberate. The question you choose on the text that you have prepared will help you to focus your response and indicate to the examiner your level of understanding of how to bring the text to life for an audience in relation to what you have been asked. The purpose of the question is to help you to focus and to recognise that you do not need to tell the examiner everything you know about the proposed production.

It is simply not enough to write as much as possible and hope to access the marks at the top end in this essay-style question. If you panic or are less well prepared than you might have been, you may resort to writing as much as possible about your concept in this section without any regard for what the question is actually demanding of you. Be careful and be warned as you read this that the examiner will only award marks for material within your answer that actually satisfies the criteria as defined in the question. A wide-ranging knowledge of the text, the playwright, the historical period and past productions, in itself, will not enable you to access the higher bands of marks. A focused and considered response will almost certainly be more beneficial, and indicate to the examiner the degree of confidence and understanding with which you have approached the question. It is not difficult to deconstruct the question and to see what it is looking for, as there are only so many aspects of performance that can be asked about in this unit. We will lead you through this process a little later in this chapter.

The Examiner says:

It might be worth taking stock at this point to consider the text your are preparing in its theatrical context and take some time to assess what you actually do know about it. The question is about what you as director would do to bring it to life for a twenty-first-century audience. Your examiner – who is, effectively, your 'audience' – is (or has recently been) a drama teacher and so will have an understanding of both the chosen text and what you are presenting as director. Your examiner is not looking to penalise you

but you do need to be aware that, at this level of study, you will be excepted to be able to explore ideas that are both relevent and appropriate to your chosen text and not simply list ideas in an unstructured, unfocused way. The unit assumes preparation, and your examiner is aware that you have your annotated copy of the script and your Live Theatre performance notes in front of you in the examination room.

POSSIBLE APPROACHES TO CONCEPTS/INTERPRETATIONS

The concept that you prepare needs to be developed and created over a period of time in the context of the text and its original performance conditions. There is no real restriction here in terms of what and how and where, but, as we have already said, there should be a degree of knowledge applied to the concept in order to ensure that it will make sense theatrically. The examiner will assess the response to the question for its knowledge and understanding of the original, and for its possible theatrical impact as presented on the page. The most successful interpretations will lift off the page and the examiner will be able to visualise immediately what is there to engage your audience. The concept that you present in relation to the question must make sense theatrically and it should draw upon the range of influences and experiences you have explored during the course. There is always a fine balance between exercising the imagination and missing the point completely, and your teacher will set out to ensure that your concept will make sense in relation to the original – and any influences you may cite – and that it will work within accepted performance conditions. If your teacher is concerned that your concept may not enable you to access the marks, then you must listen to that opinion, probably given with a series of reasons, and amend your concept accordingly. It is much better that you seek opinions before the examination in June than sit there with an idea that you will find difficult to justify in terms of the text and the question. Most teachers will not wait for you to ask an opinion about your concept; they will structure an approach to this unit that builds into the preparation time opportunities for you to share your ideas on a regular basis right up to the moment when you have to define the interpretation and fix it within your script.

The concept you develop needs to recognise the playwright's original intentions as far as you understand them. There is more to this than accessing a search engine and downloading information, although there is nothing wrong with this as a starting point in itself. Your level of understanding is developed from research into the appropriate historical time period and the general information gathered about performance conditions at the time. The more you are able to access this information and apply this knowledge to your concept, the more likely you are to be able to access the higher level of marks in the examination. There is a lot wrapped up in this, but, again, connections can be made with other units of this specification in order to remind you of what you already know and how you managed to acquire that information. You will probably be surprised, if you look back at your exploration notes for Unit 1, for example, how much information you actually have about the craft of the playwright, the influence of a practitioner and how texts may be brought to life for an audience. The experience of preparing for this section should therefore build very clearly on what has gone before and there are obvious influences that can be harnessed when looking at an interpretation. We will look at some of these in more detail a little later.

PRACTITIONERS – MAKING THE CONNECTION

In making the connection with the other units, your teacher may want to re-enforce the impact that practitioners may have had on performances in which you have been involved, and you may be encouraged to revisit the practitioner(s) explored for Unit 1. The ideas of a recognised practitioner used to support an overall concept may have an impact on the responses you are able to offer in this unit. The practitioner may not be appropriate, of course, and you will need to recognise this and be able to select an alternative if you feel this to be the case. There is no point trying to justify your concept in relation to a practitioner that you are not convinced would actually lend anything to your interpretation. It is probably better not to mention a practitioner at all than it is to try to make one fit. There is nothing to say that you must have a practitioner in mind, but this does not mean that you should not look at some ideas and methodologies and see if these could fit your concept or, indeed, inspire it.

As far as this specification from Edexcel is concerned, the word 'practitioner' covers theatre companies as well as individuals, so it may be that you have seen productions by, for example, *Northern Broadsides*, or *Out of Joint* or *Bruvvers* as part of the course. It would be useful research for you to go back into this performance practice in order to remind yourself of the possibilities for performance that may inspire you towards a concept for the chosen text. A touring theatre company by necessity has to adopt a different approach to creating theatre than a company that is based in a specific theatre and creates for that space. There are exceptions to this, but there may be more of an influence for this unit out there from companies like *Kaos* or *Hull Truck* than you might have at first thought.

This section of the examination in particular looks at the theatrical impact of the intended production, and you may need some guidance towards thinking about the possibilities and the potential within the script. While there is nothing set out in tablets of stone there is the script itself and the style and form of it as your starting point from where you can go into all kinds of other areas, with or without specific influences from practitioners. We spent some time in AS *Drama and Theatre Studies* looking at the work of specific practitioners in relation to Unit 1 and Unit 2, and it may be worth having a look at the information there as you consider your possible approach to the chosen text here. Your work in Unit 3 may also throw up some ideas for you to consider. Your teacher will have a view on practitioners and will guide you on this, but it is ultimately your concept that you will need to justify in the examination.

There is no doubt that you need to consider the use of a practitioner in your response very carefully. It could be that the ideas of a well-known practitioner, explored in relation to the overall concept and, where appropriate, within the structuring of your responses to the rehearsal process will only be of benefit to the overall impression you create within the answer. There are exceptions to this and you will need to be clear about the practitioner and your understanding of the influence on you as director that will indeed enhance your responses in section A and section B.

Examples of practitioners you could look at whose ideas might lend themselves to all three texts are Artaud, Berkoff and Brecht, along with theatre companies including those named above. There will be others, and there is nothing to say that one practitioner will fit all, but the connections across units could provide a source of inspiration for you at this point in the course, particularly if you are one of those students who may struggle with the idea of a written examination.

What your teacher may do is to set a research project that enables you in small groups to present information to the others on a range of four or five practitioners whose ideas may be appropriate for exploring in the A2 year. This could be a valuable exercise during the preparation process for Unit 4, and it may also connect very well with your work for Unit 3. Your teacher may introduce this as part of an induction programme to launch the A2 year. For you it might be a reassuring exercise in that you will realise, either in your own particular research project or in response to those from others in the group, how much you actually do know and how much of your work to date has in fact been influenced by practitioners.

Extension Activity

Exploring practitioners

In pairs, look at your exploration notes from Unit 1 and isolate those elements that may be of assistance to you in exploring the chosen Unit 4 text. You may want to structure a workshop activity for the rest of your class based on one of the written and one of the practical elements from Unit 1.

If your response to the text is influenced by a practitioner, it is not necessary for you to write in detail about the practitioner in the examination. The information you include in the answer will let the examiner know the level of your understanding of the work of the practitioner through the practical examples you will detail in the response. It does, however, need to be apparent that the practitioner has indeed influenced your directorial concept. There is no point your detailing the influence of the work of, for example, Caryl Churchill and stating this clearly in the opening paragraph of a response to this section if there is then little or no evidence of this as your response develops. The examiner is looking for you to have assimilated a range of ideas from the practitioner that has influenced decisions made for the proposed production of the chosen text. You should aim to convince the examiner through the way you select the evidence to support your response in the answer booklet.

This is a written examination and there are time constraints for which you need to prepare. There is no possibility of your writing everything you may wish to about the proposed production of the text in 50 minutes, so you will need to be selective in the information you include in your answer. The question will be the starting point for your response, followed by the information that you have in the annotated copy of the script you will have with you in the examination room. There needs to be a confidence about your response, a confidence that persuades the examiner you are choosing a few examples from the many that you could offer, only because of the time and page constraints the examination imposes upon you. The confidence comes from thorough preparation of the text and an approach to the type of questions you might expect to have to answer.

Your teacher will lead you towards structuring examination answers that will demonstrate your understanding not only of the text but also of an approach to the text that will bring it to life for an audience. There is a technique to answering examination questions in general, and there are probably a number of ideas your teacher will want to explore with you in order to help you to prepare for this question. A structured approach leading you towards June of the A2 year is probably recommended if you are going to have any chance of accessing that outstanding level of marks.

WORKED EXAMPLE

If a section B question asks you to '*explore one design element in relation to your proposed production of the chosen text*', you do need to be selective about the examples you give in support of the response. The structure to a response might look something like this:

- *Paragraph 1*: A general overview of the proposed concept, giving details of where it might be performed, the style of the performance and how this relates to the original performance conditions of the play. The final sentence of this opening concept could then connect specifically into the demands of the question:

    > My set, therefore, will be designed to show the influence of Elizabethan theatre but I am going to explore a contemporary take in my response in order to help my audience to see the relevance of the play in performance in the twenty-first century.

- *Paragraph 2*: This paragraph will then start to expand on the thinking behind the chosen design element – in this case set – and start to give some examples, supported by reasons, of the general approach to the set, expanding on the statement made at the end of the first paragraph. It might look at entrances and exits in relation to the overall concept for the proposed performance and specifically in relation to individual characters within the play – the devil being an obvious example to start with:

    > I think it is important that the set gives my actors an opportunity to move freely within it while giving it a claustrophobic feel, indicating Faustus being trapped by his life at the start of the play. Entrances and exits need to be defined and I am looking at a fairly traditional approach to this, reflecting my understanding of Elizabethan theatre conventions. I need to consider the underworld. . . .

- *Paragraph 3*: This paragraph will connect the specific examples of entrances and exits at certain moments during the production with the overall design concept as it relates to the set and how it is used, giving examples in support but avoiding simply listing all the elements of the set and how these might be used. It is important that you keep going back to the question and making sure that its specific demand is being met within the response, and paragraph 3 is a good point to remind yourself of this, as it is likely that you will turn the page and the question itself will be hidden from view.
- *Paragraph 4*: Expanding on the ideas explored in paragraph 3, provide some specific examples from key moments during the proposed production to illustrate how the set design will work for the audience and help them to see and understand your overall concept for your production. This paragraph may give information about difficulties that may have to be overcome with the chosen design element – it may explore decisions about use of colours, or it may explore the thrust stage in the production space. This paragraph may let the examiner know that some difficulty has needed to be overcome in order for the design to work in performance. It may connect with one or more other design elements with specific examples in support – lighting and coloured filters at specific times, for example.
- *Paragraph 5*: Conclusion, drawing everything together and ensuring that the question has been addressed. This paragraph should let the examiner know that you have answered the question and are able to offer some final thoughts on the chosen element in relation to the question and the proposed production. A solid, well-structured conclusion will let the examiner know that the response has been confident and considered, and has been prepared for the specific question, not simply lifted from your notes.

Your response may be structured in more than five paragraphs, depending on the way you have been prepared for the examination. This just gives you an idea of how your answer might be structured and developed in order to respond to the question. Notice that it is an immediate and personal response to the question and that you are probably going to engage with your examiner much more effectively through the use of the first person in your response.

ASSESSMENT AND MARKS

Your response to section B is worth up to 30 marks and the examiner is looking to you to be able to respond to the chosen question giving clear and practical examples in support. Your annotated copy of the script will be extremely useful but it is not the answer to the question; it provides the thinking behind the answer and needs to be seen in this context if it is to be of any value at all to you in the examination room. Do not fall into the trap of the under-prepared and simply list everything that you have in your text and hope to access some marks that way. You may be lucky and scrape some marks together at the bottom level but you need to be looking much higher than this in order to build up the points that you have already earned on the course to date.

There is no set way of preparing the chosen text for the examination but it needs to be annotated with sufficient information to make it of benefit to both section A and section B. Any annotation therefore needs to inform your responses to both of these sections. It may be that your teacher will suggest a particular approach to annotation that he or she thinks makes it easier for you to access the information more quickly under examination conditions.

If your version of the text is A4 size, with blank pages on the left as you open it up, then your teacher may encourage you to use the left-hand pages for your director's concept and the pages containing the body of the text itself on the right-hand side for your rehearsal ideas. You will know when the script is opened up in the examination room that information for section A is on the right-hand side, and information for section B is on the left. You may include a drawing/sketch of your proposed staging somewhere near the front of your script and you can copy this into your answer booklet if you feel it is appropriate to do so – and if you think it will help you to expand on your ideas more effectively.

While there may be some overlap of information throughout your text, at least you will be able to focus more effectively than if you have to leaf through a number of pages in order to gather together one set of thoughts. Any annotation should ideally be in response to practical activity around the chosen text. There may be some background information included there as well as the results of research activity, but you are not allowed to take any prepublished material into the examination. This might include:

- Theatre programmes
- Extracts from books/magazines
- Downloads
- Pictures or photographs stuck into the working copy of the script.

This version of the script is only helpful to you if it has been prepared with the questions in mind. The script might therefore contain the following:

- A family tree of the central characters and their relationship(s) with other characters in the play.
- A brief plot summary.
- A drawing/sketch of the proposed set/staging that you could copy into the answer booklet, probably in response to a section B question if appropriate.
- Drawings/sketches of costumes for central characters that can be copied into the answer booklet, probably in response to a section B question if appropriate.
- A key inside the front cover of where to find particular scenes/important moments that you may want to draw upon in order to support a response to either question. While you must respond to section A in relation to the extract that you will be given in the examination, you may have other sections of the text that you have annotated with particular rehearsal techniques and strategies that you could apply equally as well to the given extract. Section B is about bringing your interpretation to life for the audience, but you cannot write about the whole play in this response as there will not be time, so you may have some key moments of the text in mind that can be drawn upon, as appropriate, to support your answer.
- Passages of the text annotated in relation to rehearsal techniques or strategies that have been used to explore those extracts in practical workshop activities.
- Passages of the text highlighted with more detail written on the left-hand page to support your overall director's concept/interpretation of the text to bring it to life for the audience.

It is worth reminding you at this stage that everything you write in section A and section B is written with you in the role of director. You are in charge and need to demonstrate that you understand that responsibility in relation to the text, its context, your audience and the question.

14 Exploring interpretations for section B

INTERPRETATION OR CONCEPT

Section B asks you to respond to a focus question on the chosen text using the concept or interpretation you have prepared. Students sometimes wonder about the words 'interpretation' and 'concept' and how – and if – they are different. For the purposes of this examination your teacher may use these two words interchangeably with you. For example:

> *The interpretation of the text in order to bring it to life for your audience will lead you to define a concept in your text.*

Or your teacher might say:

> *Your concept should enable you to express ideas for your audience to show an understanding of the text and how to bring it to life for your audience in an interpretation of the original.*

Either way, the task you face before you go into the examination room is exactly the same. You know you are in the role of director and you know that you will be asked a question which will help you to focus your thoughts and demonstrate your understanding of how a director may bring a text to life for an audience. The interpretation or concept of the chosen text must remain true to the playwright's original intentions. Apart from that, there are no other rules about this and there are no rights and wrongs that your examiner will be looking for. The main consideration you need to have is whether or not what you are defining in your response will actually make theatrical sense to your audience. In this chapter we will look at some ideas for how you might arrive at an interpretation for each of the three texts available for this unit.

GENERAL POINTS ON INTERPRETATIONS

While there is no long list of rules attached to this there are things you need to consider when arriving at your interpretation. Your teacher will guide you further on this, but you need to be aware of the following as a starting point:

- Any interpretation needs to make sense when seen in relation to the original text.
- You can be as imaginative and as creative as you like, but the interpretation needs to work within accepted and recognisable theatrical conventions.
- Your interpretation may be inspired by and make reference to the work of a recognised theatre practitioner, but it does not have to do this if you feel you want to draw upon other experiences in your ideas.
- The starting point for your interpretation may be an incident or character or theme that you want to bring out for your audience and you may focus on this by editing the text in an appropriate way.
- Updating the original to a modern setting is acceptable but you need to make sure that your update makes sense when compared to the original and places it into a recognisable context for the audience without taking anything away from the playwright's original intentions so far as we are aware of them.
- While it is your interpretation, you need to have your examiner in mind since it is the examiner you will have to convince in relation to the question that has been set. What may make sense among your group of friends may not make sense in the bigger picture of the examination.
- Your interpretation does not have to be different from everybody else's but it does need to make sense to you, as you are the person who needs to be able to write about it in the examination.

You need to be confident enough to be able to respond to the focus question and you will have your interpretation set out in the annotated copy of the text that you can take into the examination with you. This copy of the text and your annotation is not the answer to the question but it should support what you are going to write if you are able to access the information quickly and clearly in the examination.

GETTING STARTED

The starting point for your interpretation has to be the text in its Edexcel version. There are other versions published for all three texts available for this unit, and it may be that you explore one or two of these to give you more of an overview of the version you need to use in the examination. There is no requirement for you to do this and, indeed, your teacher may steer you clear of this, but you may find it useful as an extension activity. Be careful though of getting confused. Other versions of *Woyzeck*, for example, have scenes in a different order, and you will need to be careful that you are writing about the Edexcel version in the examination.

Consider the following and see how helpful this list might be in guiding your thinking around your interpretation.

WORKED EXAMPLE

When preparing for section A and section B:

- How do you set about demonstrating an understanding of the play and its original context?
- What do you think is the relevance of the play in the twenty-first century?
- How might you set about helping your audience to make connections between their lives and the lives of the characters in your interpretation of the chosen text?
- How might you arrive at your own directorial interpretation and what strategies might you use to help you to work with actors and designers to realise this interpretation?
- What is your understanding of the nature and purpose of rehearsals and how does this understanding connect into your overall interpretation?
- Consider how you can acquire a 'toolbox' of rehearsal techniques and where you might find this information to support you.

You cannot set out on the directorial path without considering what your purpose is as director. There is a responsibility as director for you to sympathetically bring the work of the playwright to life for your audience and you have a responsibility to your audience to ensure that their experience is as far as possible a theatrical event that offers them something new in the twenty-first century based on the original. The following questions may help you to guide your thinking.

WORKED EXAMPLE

- What is the intended experience for the audience?
- What themes do you want to highlight and emphasise?
- Do you intend to raise questions in the minds of the audience?
- Do you want to engage the audience in an exploration?
- Is your intention to give the audience a message?
- Is the primary function of your production to entertain the audience?
- How do you want the audience to feel and what do you want them to think about as they leave the performance?
- How will your production help the audience see the relevance of this play in the twenty-first century?

A useful exercise right at the start of the preparation process might be to try to come up with the most outrageous and ridiculous interpretation of the chosen text as you can think of and share this with the class. Once you have been through this, you can then focus more clearly on the interpretation that will take the original and shape a response that demonstrates your understanding of it through your intended performance.

TO UPDATE OR NOT TO UPDATE

There is a real temptation here to want to update the chosen text in order to make it relevant for your chosen audience. First, if you think about this, you do not need to update the text in order to achieve the relevance. If the material is relevant then it will be so, however you may think of staging it. To be clear about this, you cannot change the words of the playwright, so any update needs to be achieved through other means, not through changing the text other than cutting and editing if and when appropriate. You cannot change character names or names of places, for example, to reference locations close to where you may be performing the piece, but you can edit out sections that you feel are not relevent to your interpretation. Second, it is never a good idea to underestimate your audience. In this case your actual audience is an examiner sitting in front of a screen reading your response, but you do need to keep a live audience in mind in your planning in order for you to try to visualise your interpretation and a reaction to it in performance.

When they write about *updating the play*, most students mean that they are looking at the visual experience for the audience with an interpretation that sets it in a recognisable twenty-first-century arena. This is fine so long as the chosen visual references make sense for the interpretation of the play as a whole and in relation to its original context. You do, of course, need to be aware of its original context, and your research needs to inform any decision you make about an interpretation for a twenty-first-century audience. You cannot ignore the roots of the play, in the same way as you cannot ignore the playwright's original intentions; both are connected and need to be linked in your interpretation. Whichever play you are working on for Unit 4, you must have an understanding of its social, cultural, historical and political context.

15 The texts for section A and section B

A BRIEF OVERVIEW

Each of these texts has its own particular challenges for you in the role of director. Whether you are presented with the text that you and your group will be studying or you are given more of a choice by your teacher, the final decision must be made to enable you to access the marks and to draw on the skills you have developed throughout this course. Your whole group must study the same text (even though other groups in your school or college may be studying one of the other texts), and the more practical your approach is to the text, the more likely it will be that you will be able to access the marks for this unit. We have identified the following five areas as possible major challenges for you across all three texts and you will need to be carefully guided in your approaches in order to meet these challenges:

- Language and meaning.
- Historical context and intention.
- Material and subject matter.
- Structure and plot.
- Accessibility for a twenty-first-century audience.

We will look at these challenges in more detail in this chapter and suggest approaches to the texts to enable you to access the marks in the written examination. There is nothing here that a student of drama and theatre studies at this level should not be able to have thoughts or opinions about.

The following brief overviews of each of the three texts give you some idea of the basic plots but offer no indication of the style and form of each text. Your research needs to place the text your teacher chooses into its historical context and research needs to be undertaken into the other two time periods to help you prepare for section C.

Aristophanes, *Lysistrata* (411 BC)

The city-states of Athens and Sparta have been at war with each other for around 20 years and Lysistrata has called together the women of Greece to force the men to stop fighting. Lysistrata has two ideas to bring about peace: one is to persuade all Greek women to withhold sexual favours from their husbands, and the other is to seize the Acropolis, where all the money of the state is kept, so that the rulers will be unable to pay the army. The women eventually agree to the sex strike and they swear an oath together. The old men of Athens attempt to recapture the Acropolis, but they soon retreat when the women pour water over them. A city magistrate attempts to reclaim the Acropolis, but he is humbled when the women dress him up in their feminine clothing and treat him like a corpse at a funeral.

Lysistrata expresses concern that many of her followers are beginning to weaken and slip away to see their husbands. She persuades them to continue with their sex strike. A young soldier, Cinesias, experiences growing sexual frustration as his wife, Myrrhine, teases him with the promise of sex, only to withdraw it when he refuses to agree to peace. Finally, an ambassador from Sparta arrives to discuss terms for peace with the Athenians. The men are unable to agree, and Lysistrata uses the presence of a naked woman (the personification of Reconciliation) as a distraction to broker a peace treaty. The play ends in a celebration of song and dance.

Christopher Marlowe, *Doctor Faustus* (*c.*1580)

Doctor Faustus, a distinguished teacher at the University of Wittenberg in Germany, declares his dissatisfaction with academic learning and decides to devote himself to the study of magic. He summons up the evil spirit Mephistopheles, and proposes a contract (later signed in his blood) in which he trades his soul for 24 years during which time Mephistopheles will be his servant, answer all his questions and give him whatever he wants. Mephistopheles gives him a book containing the secrets of the universe. Later, Faustus has doubts, but despite being urged by the Good Angel is unable to repent. Lucifer appears and distracts him with a parade of the Seven Deadly Sins. Faustus (invisibly) visits the Pope's court where he mocks and plays practical jokes on him. He visits the Emperor of Constantinople and 'resurrects' Alexander the Great for him. Later, after playing a practical joke on a horse-dealer, he 'resurrects' Helen of Troy for three fellow scholars.

In the final scene, which takes place during the last hour of the 24 years, Faustus is struck with terror at the thought of his eternal damnation, but cannot bring about his own repentance. After the clock strikes midnight, devils appear to drag him off to hell.

Georg Buchner, *Woyzeck* (1879)

Franz Woyzeck is a soldier who has fathered an illegitimate son with his girlfriend, Marie. He is a poor man and has a soldier friend called Andres. There is a fairground scene involving animals and a Showman, and Marie becomes very taken with a Drum-Major.

Woyzeck earns extra pay by working for a Captain who finds him stupid and amoral because he is poor. He thinks a poor man could never be virtuous. Woyzeck also agrees to take part in paid medical experiments carried out on him by the Doctor. For one of these, the Doctor tells Woyzeck he must eat nothing except peas in order to prove some unspecified scientific theory. Woyzeck begins to lose his sanity, has a series of visions and suffers from paranoia. The Doctor parades him in front of his students, convincing everyone that Woyzeck is going insane as a result of his female upbringing, using the German language and the diet of peas.

Meanwhile, Marie begins an affair with the Drum-Major. She eventually gives in to him in an ambiguous scene that could disguise her actual rape. The Captain informs Woyzeck of Marie's indiscretions. Woyzeck confronts Marie in a rage. He is driven even more angry when he sees Marie and her lover dancing together, and eventually starts to hear voices telling him to stab her. The Drum-Major beats up Woyzeck in a fight.

Woyzeck buys a knife from a Jewish merchant. He lures Marie to the woods and stabs her, but is quickly found out because he is covered in blood. He runs back to her body and takes it to a nearby pool, then presumably drowns.

The Doctor carries out post-mortem examinations on both of the bodies, and finds that Woyzeck's corpse has no blood left in it. When Andres returns to the woods where Woyzeck dies, he finds the ground running with blood. He is visited in the mist-shrouded scene by the grandmother, who provides a presence in the mist as Andres runs off.

MAKING THE CHOICE

There are a number of factors to be considered here, not least of which is the choice of performance you will see for section C. This will have an impact on the choice of text you work with for sections A and B.

Unit 4 is about three distinct periods in theatrical history with a focus on the theatre of Ancient Greece, the Elizabethan period and the nineteenth century. Your work in this unit must cover two of these three theatrical periods, one in the text chosen to explore for section A and B and the other in the choice of play seen for section C.

The specification defines the periods of theatrical development as follows:

- 525 BC–AD 65
- 1564–1720
- 1828–1914.

Have a look at the following combinations of texts and given periods, and the permissible combinations will become more clear for you. In section C you do not need to see a production of the given text from the chosen period, but a production of any play written and performed between the given dates is acceptable.

Sections A and B: text explored	*Section C: given time period*
Lysistrata	Either 1564–1720 or 1828–1914
Doctor Faustus	Either 525 BC–AD 65 or 1828–1914
Woyzeck	Either 525 BC–AD 65 or 1564–1720

Extension Activity

Important plays and playwrights from the three time periods specified in Unit 4

- Research each of the three time periods covered in Unit 4 and list, for each, the names of five major playwrights and the titles of three of their best-known plays.
- Access local and national theatre listings and see which, if any, of the plays on your list are available to you in performance.

16 The role of director in section A and section B

THE DIRECTOR

director
The person in control of all aspects of the production, primarily in relation to the actors but also responsible for the ideas to inspire the design considerations to support the overall vision. Most directors will work collaboratively but will exercise the right to have the final say.

In this unit, the director is paramount. In sections A and B you are in the role of director for an interpretation of the chosen text, and in section C you are responding to a director's interpretation of a text as an informed member of an audience. Whether you are the director, or you are recognising the impact a director may have in bringing a play to life for an audience, you need to have a rounded understanding of what a director is responsible for in the creative process from first reading to opening night and, in many cases, beyond. Your examiner will expect you to be able to use appropriate language, terms and expressions to support your responses and for you to have gained a clear understanding of the function of the director from other aspects of the course. There is more to this unit than recognising the work of a director; you need to be able to apply your ideas to your proposed rehearsal and performance of the chosen text in sections A and B, and you need to be able to define what it is that a director has brought to a twenty-first-century interpretation of the text for section C that may – or may not – be connected back into its original performance conditions.

It may be that your interpretation has been influenced by work you have seen or been involved in, and there is a real skill in taking something that has inspired you and adapting those ideas for your own purposes in your role as director. There is nothing wrong in being influenced by others. The Arts are littered with great artists across all of the disciplines whose work has been influenced and inspired by the work of others.

Extension Activity

The craft of the director

We have listed three directors here who are currently working in the UK and creating theatre that is distinctive and, at times, challenging for audiences.

In this research task, choose one of the directors from the following list and find out what you can about her or his approach to creating the experience for the audience that is distinctive and could be said to be the trademark of that director.

The three directors are:

- Katie Mitchell
- Emma Rice
- Greg Doran.

Once you have carried out your research, try to distil into no more than five bullet points what you might consider to be the essential approach of your chosen director and, with your own work in mind, weigh up how relevent this kind of approach may be in relation to your own interpretation of the chosen text. There are no rights or wrongs to this. You may feel that your research leads you to conclude that your chosen director is not at all influential for the text or for your approach to it. If this is the case, you will need to widen your research activity.

FUNCTION OF THE DIRECTOR

You could probably debate this point in your group for hours if you wanted to and there may be an opportunity in the A2 year structure for you to explore this at some length in a session. For every point you agree with, there may be another that you feel is not really part of your vision of the function of the director. Any list, however broad and inclusive, will also exclude something that you or your teacher may feel is important, so we offer the following list as a starting point rather than a defining moment in your planning. It is a generic list to which you may add specific directorial functions in relation to the chosen text.

The function of the director is:

- To have a concept of the play in terms of style and setting.
- To conceive an interpretation.

- To be responsible for the process with the company.
- To challenge preconceptions but to be aware of the source material.
- To facilitate ownership for the actors within a structured approach to rehearsals.
- To provide an outside eye.
- To enable everyone to contribute but to know when to make a final decision.
- To enable actors and designers to contribute to the interpretation but to always have the concept in mind.
- To raise questions.
- To tell everybody what to do.
- To enable the actors and designers to understand the play and the interpretation that will lead to the performance.
- To be a time manager and to stay focused.
- To motivate.
- To plan and structure rehearsal tasks and techniques.
- To be able to communicate with actors and designers.
- To be able to experiment and explore with actors in order to widen and deepen the interpretation of the play.
- To plan and run rehearsals.
- To be a leader.

When you look at this list closely, you will see that there is some overlap of ideas in some of the statements and there are some contradictions here too. If, for example, as director, you are telling everybody what to do, how can you also be experimenting and exploring with actors? It may be that you look at this list and select the five most relevant statements that could inform your approach to section A and section B and then add to the five generic statements five others that are specific to your chosen text. You may want to highlight:

- To explore choral speech and movement

as part of your approach as director of an interpretation of *Lysistrata*, for example. There is no specific mention of audience in this list at the moment and you may feel that you need to be more focused as director on your intended impact on your audience, certainly as far as creating a response to an examination question is concerned, and you may want to add to your own list something like:

- To be aware of the intended impact of the performance on the audience

You may also decide that you want to be more specific about design in relation to preparing your text for performance and you may want to subdivide design into its component parts in order to help you to focus on something you think is going to be really important for your interpretation. You may want, for example:

- To explore the use of mask in relation to chorus

if you are looking at *Lysistrata*, or you may want:

- To explore the use of colour in light and costume

in relation to a production of *Doctor Faustus*.

Directors all have different ways of working, and a good director will probably adopt a range of methods in order to bring out the best in his or her company at any one time during the rehearsal process but always with the performance in mind. There is no point being an excellent and creative rehearsal director if this does not lead to a performance that is engaging for your audience. There have probably never been any reviews that have contained the line:

> **Pity about the performance but the rehearsals were excellent**

As director in this unit, you need to give confident responses to the questions that will let your examiner know that you have understood the role of director in the theatre and have been able to adapt that generic vision to your own interpretation of the chosen text. It is not about the director, it is about you as the director.

THE DIRECTOR IN REHEARSAL

Section A is about you as director responding to an extract from the text with a three-part focus question that will ask you to detail how you would plan a rehearsal of the extract to enable your actors and designers to develop their contributions to the eventual performance. As the director, it is expected that you will have ideas in place for suitable and appropriate rehearsal techniques that you feel will enable your company to respond to the text. These techniques may or may not be referenced to a specific practitioner but, whether they are or whether they are not, you need to be able to justify your methods within your answer. Consider the list of rehearsal techniques that follows and look at how many of them, or variations of them, you are familiar with:

- Characters tell the story of their life and/or key moments in their life in the present or past tense.

- Character as an animal/flower.
- Identify everything a character says about him/herself, and everything that is said by others about that character.
- Working on a section of text, 'translate' and perform it in contemporary language.
- Improvise scenes depicting events that happened before the play starts.
- Identify the images the playwright uses and represent them physically while the dialogue is spoken.
- One actor speaks the first line of an extract and throws a ball to another; whoever has the ball speaks the next line.
- Physical activities that help a chorus to act and move as one body. In pairs the actors move around the room, and in changing their movement they should try to change as one. The size of the group gradually increases until the whole group is moving together.
- Working on a short section of text, each actor identifies the active verbs that are most appropriate in achieving their objective in relationship to other characters, at any given time. The choice of verbs then informs the physical and vocal interaction between characters.

Extension Activity

Rehearsal techniques

Consider the above list of rehearsal techniques and choose three that you think could be useful to you in relation to the chosen text.

Add to your list of three another three techniques you may have come across in other areas of the course that you feel could give you six techniques in total which may be useful for you to put together a rehearsal for a section or scene from the chosen text.

Within your group it may be a good idea to share your list of six techniques and see how much overlap there is, but, more importantly, what others have on their lists that you do not and to see if those ideas could add something to your own list.

THE PURPOSE OF REHEARSAL

As director, you will need to have in mind a rehearsal structure but you also need to be clear about what the purpose of rehearsal is. There is the obvious here, but consider the list that follows and see how far it echoes your own thoughts.

Some functions of rehearsal might include:

- Exploration of themes.
- Enabling the actors and/or designers to understand and realise the interpretation.
- Exploration of the playwright's intentions.
- Character exploration and interpretation.
- Character relationships.
- Developing an understanding of the social, cultural, political and historical context.
- Development of vocal skills.
- Work on proxemics, movement and gesture.
- Work on style and language.
- Exploration of the use of costume.
- Function and portrayal of individual characters and the ensemble of the piece.

Extension Activity

The purpose of rehearsal

Consider the list of functions of rehearsal. It is not exhaustive, and you may wish to add to it in order to make it complete in your own experience.

Consider your own approach to the chosen text and choose one of the functions of rehearsal from this list and add to it at least two rehearsal techniques you think would be appropriate in order for you to deliver your intentions during that rehearsal. Use the following example to give you an idea of how to approach this:

- *Function*: To work on the style and language.
- *Rehearsal techniques*: Working on a section of text, 'translate' and perform it in contemporary language.
- Identify the images the playwright uses and represent them physically while the dialogue is spoken.

THE DIRECTOR AND THE INTERPRETATION

We explore this in some detail in Chapter 13 on exploring interpretations. You should be very clear about your ideas, however, and there needs to be a confidence in your response to section B in the examination booklet that allows your examiner to feel your confidence from the way you express yourself in the written response. The examiner will assume that you have had preparation time and that any response you offer is considered and is a result of research and practical activity around the chosen text. It will need to make theatrical sense and probably draw from other experiences you may have had in other aspects of the course. The examination room is not the time for you to be thinking about your interpretation and whether or not it will work in reality. The time for this kind of thinking is in the preparation process where you should be given the opportunity to explore your ideas within the group and to workshop some of those ideas with your group to give you a sense of how they might work in both rehearsal and performance.

ACCESSING THE QUESTIONS

There will never be a question on the examination paper that starts with the following phrase:

Tell us everything you know about. . . .

The questions will tend to be much more focused than this and you need to be prepared to structure your response to demonstrate what you have planned, as well as to give some examples from your rehearsal strategies in section A and from your interpretation in section B.

As director, you have overall control of the interpretation and have the final say on all aspects of the production. You are therefore responsible. In the examination the focus questions will be looking for you to have taken your responsibility seriously, and you need to be able to demonstrate this in your confident responses to the rehearsal and performance questions. Every aspect of the production needs to be prepared just in case there is an opportunity to write about it in the examination. However, as in productions themselves, sometimes less is more, and you may find that you do not need to give all the information you have because either it is not relevent to the question or there is neither time nor space for you to be able to do so. As director, you will have created an annotated copy of the text that will cover rehearsal and performance and will inform your thinking in the examination room. It will not provide the answers to the questions, but it will point you in the right direction and give you some clear examples to draw upon as and when appropriate. You are almost going into the examination in role as director, and you are thinking yourself into that state of mind in order to be able to respond positively to the questions.

17 Annotating the text

ANNOTATION

In this chapter we will look at annotation and what this may mean for you in relation to the chosen text. There is a state in which you could find yourself that you need to avoid as far as possible, and this state is represented by two extremes. These are:

- Too much annotation and you do not know where to start when it comes to finding information to support your response to the question.
- Too little annotation and you do not know where to start when it comes to finding information to support your response to the question.

You need to have annotation that supports your responses to both section A and section B. For section A the annotation needs to focus on rehearsal and for section B you need to have information that will support your response to the question about your interpretation or concept for the play in performance. The annotation needs to be easily accessible under examination conditions and must be written into the text itself; you are not allowed to insert pictures, drawings or photographs.

A well-placed drawing or sketch

In all cases, whichever text you are bringing to life in the examination it is probably a good idea to have a drawing of your proposed staging on the first available blank page in your script that you can then copy into your examination paper where appropriate, probably in response to section B. A well-placed drawing or diagram, even at A level, can be really supportive to your writing as long as you are able to refer to it in the body of your answer as well. If you are able to attract your examiner's eye to the drawing to develop a staging point you are making, this could be extremely useful, as it aids the examiner's understanding and demonstrates that you have considered this point in enough detail to supply a diagram to demonstrate it. There is no point, however, in illustrating your work with pointless sketches that are not referred to in your answer and are only there to provide a decorative background. You might include sketches of costumes or particular scenes to show proxemics, for example. These do not have to be elaborate or necessarily well drawn but they do need to illustrate the point you are making in order for them to be meaningful for your examiner. You could have some examples already in the body of your text arising from workshops around particular sections and it could be these that you use to support your answers.

Everything you put into your answer must be there for a purpose and to provide evidence of your understanding for your examiner. There are two sides to this understanding: the first is that you have understood the text; the second is that you have understood the question and have therefore provided what you think is appropriate evidence in support of your response from your prepared text.

Include an index

You might include an index of important scenes and exchanges between characters at the front of your script. The examination is not a test of memory, which is why you are allowed to take the text in with you. It is a test of understanding the role of director, and your director's copy of the script will include a breakdown of key scenes and moments and where to find them at the front of your text, making it easier to access the information should you need it to support either section in the examination.

Rehearsal techniques and methods

Your script might be annotated with specific examples of rehearsal techniques and methods associated with scenes from the play that you have explored in practical workshop activities. These annotations are often useful, as they will draw you back to the practical activity and help you to re-create them for your examiner in the response to a section A question. Even if the question refers to a different part of the play, the rehearsal techniques you used in your preparation may still be relevent, or they may remind you of other techniques you can then apply in relation to the extract that you are given in the examination. Depending on the number of workshops you are involved in as part of the preparation for Unit 4, you may have a number of extracts that are annotated to a lesser or greater degree. These can be useful to you as reminders of that practical activity, and will provide a way of including information in your script that is relevent.

Your concept or interpretation

It may be useful to use the blank pages to the left of your script to develop your ideas for your concept or interpretation, and to include examples on these pages of how you think your ideas will work in reality. You do not need to cover every page of your text and you do not need to have specific examples in mind for every aspect of your proposed production. What you might have as part of your annotation is an overarching statement at the front of your script that succinctly provides the focus of your interpretation and then some key moments of your choice from within the body of the text that will help you to demonstrate how the concept might work in reality in relation to a number of chosen performance elements. You may have ideas about how particular scenes may work in performance from the point of view of performer and designer, and how you intend to impact on the audience using appropriate elements of the theatre.

Historical context

Your annotation may include references to the historical context of the play and some examples of how scenes may have been staged in the original performance conditions and how characters may have been portrayed. The importance of this is that it will support your response by giving you information on making the necessary connections that may be relevent in your answer, particularly to section B. If you are thinking of staging your interpretation of *Doctor Faustus*, for example, in traverse, you will need to keep this in mind in relation to how it would have been presented in its original performance. For *Lysistrata* you may explore some of the conventions of Greek comedy in relation to the chorus and the use of phallic symbols, for example, but then decide on a version that deconstructs the chorus. You need to have explored the conventions before deciding how far you intend to go with them. Some of this exploration may be in your script and you may find reference points for it in your response to a question.

18 The demands of section C

Section C of Unit 4 is about you responding to one of the three historical time periods as detailed in the specification. The focus of the section is a live production of a play written and performed in the chosen time period and seen in relation to your response to it in the twenty-first century.

The live performance is at the centre of the response and you will need to reflect upon this in relation to the original performance conditions of the play. This will demand a degree of research and you will need to work in a structured approach to this section that enables you to confidently relate an experience as an audience member in the twenty-first century with the experience as you understand it of theatre in the chosen time period. While your research is important, this question is not intended to be solely historically based. It is intended to draw out from you an understanding of how theatre may be shaped for a specific audience in a specified time period and how the expectations of an audience may have altered over time. The influence of the director and decisions in relation to production values will help you to frame responses to the performance seen and offer opportunities for comparisons to be made with the original performance conditions.

There is an expectation that the vast majority of high-scoring responses will be those that present an integrated approach to the answer, moving between time periods in relation to the demands of the question. You need to think about this at an early stage in the preparation process, and you need to look to your teacher to offer you some examples of how this integrated approach may be achieved.

It is probably the case that those who present a response that is separated between the 'now' and the 'then' will probably struggle to meet the demands of the question. This integrated idea will be explored further in the assessment section for this unit, and the examples given there indicate the kind of approach that may help you to access the higher bands of marks.

There is a choice of two questions in this section and you will need to weigh up the demands of each question carefully in order to be able to access the marks. Consider:

Figure 18.1
Joanna Lumley and Annabel Scholey in Anton Chekhov's *The Cherry Orchard*, first performed in 1904. This production ran at the Sheffield Crucible in 2007

- What is the question looking for?
- What information do I have in order to be able to answer the question?
- Which of the two questions does my information suit better?

It is simply not enough for you to write as much as possible and hope to access the marks at the top end in this essay-style question. A focused and considered response will almost certainly be more beneficial.

The examiner needs to see evidence of your making the necessary connections between the live performance that you have seen and the historical period of the play's original performance in order to be able to access the higher band of marks. The question provides the connection between you, the performance seen and the Examination Board. It needs to be explored in relation to the theatrical experience and your understanding of this in relation to the historical context.

As an A level student there is an expectation that you will know the names of central performers, designers and director in relation to the production seen, and be able to reference theatrical terms and concepts with confidence and understanding in your response to section C. There should be no sense of you struggling with terminology that should be familiar to you from other units in this specification. It is not enough, for example, for you to write about '*the actor who played . . .*' or '*the costume designer had interesting ideas for . . .*' without offering names as appropriate. It would be more worrying, perhaps, if you were to write about the characters and the story of the play seen in performance, rather than about the actors and the way the performance was brought to life by the company.

It is worth your while looking at the Level 5 criteria in the mark scheme in order for you to understand what is required here and you may want to highlight words and phrases that will need attention. The sooner this kind of work can be done in the preparation process the better, as practice responses will start to become almost second nature in relation to this. You do not need to wait for your teacher to do this with you, but it could be something that you could do in pairs, perhaps with your Unit 2 buddy from last year. Once you understand the mechanics of the question you are then more able to concentrate on the creative elements of the answer, and not worry about whether or not you are getting it right with terminology and technical terms.

There are at least four basic steps your teacher can take with you to help to prepare for this section of Unit 4. Your teacher could set a research task for you in groups in order to lead seminar sessions around aspects of the appropriate historical time period. A teaching group of 12, for example, could be divided into four research groups of three, each of which can be given a different focus for their research.

- *Group 1*: Society at the time
- *Group 2*: Politics at the time
- *Group 3*: The theatre at the time
- *Group 4*: The playwright in context

There will be some overlap in the material presented but the research of each group could lead to a presentation lasting about ten minutes, with opportunities for questions. Each of the four presentations will yield a composite picture of the chosen period that forms the collective experience of the teaching group that will in turn lead the individuals in your group to compile notes under headings that may be helpful for the examination.

- Prepare for the live production. This will probably be a session looking at the play and sharing expectations of the production before going to see it, with your teacher pointing out elements of the performance for you to look out for.
- A teacher-led evaluation session after the performance, drawing out relevent material that you could include in their notes.
- You could be set written work on a regular basis that will help you to build up an approach to evaluating the live performance and to make connections to its historical perspective.

The main focus of the historical perspective is the play seen live in relation to its original context. The theatrical experience of the audience is essential here, with research into the chosen period centred on expectations and where those expectations were likely to have been founded. Any theatrical period needs to be contextualised; it is not possible to see developments in style and content in isolation, but they need to be placed – as simply as possible – into the theatrical curve. The historical perspective is essential in this unit, as it will help you to focus a response to the present with specific reference to the past, and to demonstrate your understanding of the place the play may have in its historical context. It is possible for a broad-sweep approach to research to be compartmentalised by you in order to give specific examples that might be useful to support observations made in your answers. A specific comment about the use of costume in the production seen live, for example, may then be expanded within the historical perspective to include your observations on the general use of costume in the relevant time period and any particular conventions on colour, style or character use that may be relevant.

THE ROLE OF THE TEACHER IN THE PREPARATION PROCESS

It is important that you see a live production of the play that will give you every opportunity of accessing the available marks. This is not always as straightforward as it may seem and, geographically, it is not always easy to see quality live theatre for a price that is reasonable or affordable. The intention is that the production must be seen live, and this needs to be at the forefront of the planning for this unit. Ideally, the production should be seen close to the examination date, but not so close that you do not have enough opportunities to explore the live experience, the historical perspective and the possible questions in the examination paper. Your teacher will probably be looking for opportunities to book productions right from the start of the A2 year and you need to keep your eyes open too for potential productions. It may be that your teacher hands over responsibility for finding a suitable production to you or to somebody else in your group, and this is a great opportunity for you to get involved in this important area of your course. You may even decide to book to see two or three productions over a period of time so that you and your group can have a wider range of experiences to draw from in other aspects of your course, as well as focusing on Unit 4. A word of caution here, however: your response to section C must be based on one live performance only of a play written and performed from the specified time period, not on a range of performances that you may have seen. Some productions will lend themselves to this unit better than others but you have no way of knowing this before you book, so, by choosing to go in February or March of the A2 year, for example, you will still have two or three months to find an alternative if this is necessary, should the production you have seen not be helpful in meeting the criteria of the questions.

There is no requirement that you see a production by the Royal Shakespeare Company or at the National Theatre, although it is very exciting if you are able to go to see well-established and reputable companies performing. In recent times very high-profile actors have taken on the classics. You may have been fortunate to see Ralph Fiennes as Oedipus at the National, David Tennant as Hamlet with the RSC, Patrick Stewart as Prospero with the RSC, Jude Law as Hamlet at the Donmar Warehouse, or Ian McKellan as Lear, again with the RSC. There will always be established actors who will want to tread the boards and go back to, as they see it, the roots of the acting profession. If you are fortunate enough to be present at such an event, then this would be a major bonus indeed. If not, then no matter – the play's the thing!

Any live theatre experience should provide valuable information to support your responses to questions, and this includes non-professional productions. There are a number of excellent touring companies still operating in the United Kingdom and still bringing exciting and innovative productions to theatres and other venues across the country. Some companies will perform in your school or college hall, usually for an agreed fee and a share of the box-office. It is worth your while exploring possibilities with your teacher and doing some research into what is available that may enable you to meet the requirements for Unit 4 without it costing a great deal of money. It is, of course, understandable that you want to see quality work (whatever that may mean to you in the context of this unit) but this is not always possible, particularly when you are looking at a production of a play originally written and performed within a specific time period. Your teacher has a role to play here, which is to set up the opportunity and to lead you through the process in order to help to prepare you for the demands of the question. It is also the case that you need to have opportunities to practise for the questions and to have your responses marked in order to give you an idea of what you need to be doing if you wish to be heading towards the best possible mark in the unit.

STRATEGIES FOR EXPLORING STAGING CONDITIONS

You could draw on experiences within your own centre in creating performances within specific spaces for this unit and you could reference these in relation to the performance style you see in the live piece for section C alongside its likely original performance conventions. The published facts of the historical period are the published facts, and these are at the core of the material that forms the basis for notes you will be taking into the examination. You could create your own drawings or diagrams of the main different staging configurations and explore these with specific plays in mind to see if they would work for all play types and, to some extent, across the time periods.

This kind of activity is useful for section C, but it also effectively connects into the demands of the first two sections, as it may encourage you to think about your staging alongside original conventions but also with a twenty-first-century audience in mind.

BEFORE YOU GO – PREPARING FOR THE LIVE PERFORMANCE

You may feel that it is important to read the play before you go to see it. This is not essential. There is a danger here that responses across this unit will be to the text of the play rather than to its performance. This is particularly true if you have studied the text in English, for example.

It is probably sufficient for your teacher to talk you through the main elements of the play and, perhaps, to give you a brief synopsis before you go to see it. You might collect reviews from local and national press and have a look at these too before you go or, at least, keep them in a folder for afterwards so you can make some comparisons with what the professional reviewer thought of the production.

The Examiner says:

The internet is a great source of information on theatre productions and you need to be looking at appropriate websites on a regular basis, keeping in touch with what is going on in the theatrical world, particularly if you are preparing for auditions. Students will often write about their great interest in theatre and their passion for performance in their applications, but this often means that they have appeared in a school or college production and followed the A level course but have not taken their interest beyond the institution. The specification gives you the opportunity to take your knowledge and interest beyond what you are being taught and to develop your own portfolio of material to support your interests as well as your responses in Unit 4. We are looking for a confidence in the answers, and this confidence often comes from wider reading beyond the immediate of the workshop experience.

You might carry out some research into the theatre company and/or director and discuss your ideas as to what the production might look and sound like based on your general knowledge of the company, the space and the play itself. A production of *King Lear* by The Royal Shakespeare Company, for example, is likely to be a different experience from a production of the same play by a touring company. Steven Berkoff's directorial influence on an ancient Greek text in performance is likely to be a radical departure when seen in relation to a production directed by Peter Hall.

It is probably a good idea to have a historical sense of the play in mind before the performance so it may be that a little time may be spent contextualising it and perhaps researching other productions from other time periods. This will help you to have an overall feel for what might be expected and how this might relate to its original performance conditions. There will be no requirement in the examination, however, to refer to any previous productions of the play you see live, other than the experience you have had in the context of the play's original performance conditions.

Extension Activity

Research and reminder task

1. The Royal Shakespeare Company
2. Steven Berkoff
3. Peter Hall

Use the internet to find out what you can about the above and condense your information into three five-minute presentations.

Some teachers will ask members of your group to focus on different elements as you are watching the performance. You may be asked to focus on the use of costume in the performance, another member of your group the use of light, somebody else the acting style/technique of the actors playing specific characters. You are all watching the performance, but you will each have something specific to gather information about for the discussion afterwards. During the follow-up sessions, individual students can then lead the discussion based on their specific element and help in shaping the notes for the others. You will still be watching the production but you will have a specific focus in mind, and this could help you and your group in the overall shaping of your understanding of the theatrical experience. If the size of your group allows, your teacher might consider buying seats in different areas of the auditorium and splitting the group between the different areas, perhaps swapping at the interval. This will give you an opportunity to see the performance from different spaces and to consider your reaction as an informed member of the audience in relation to this. This could be of particular interest in a space like The Royal Exchange Theatre in Manchester which is in the round with vertical tiers of seats, each level giving a different perspective on the production. Looking into the eyes of Creon as he carries the body of his dead son across the space is a different experience for you sitting at floor level from that enjoyed by other members of your group sitting on the second tier and looking down on events during a production of *Antigone* by Sophocles, for example. It may be useful for you to have a notebook and pen to hand to record information before and after the performance. Taking notes during the performance itself is distracting to others and disrespectful to the production company, but immediate responses are often helpful in forming judgements and will jog the memory later. You could make a quick sketch of the set before the production begins if the auditorium configuration allows you to do so, and you could certainly make some notes during any interval.

There is a skill to being a member of an audience, particularly at a live event as opposed to the cinema experience. You will be viewing the performance with Unit 4 in mind and you are there as an informed member of that audience. You have a role to play in making sure that the group has an overall impression of the experience to inform your own individual response that you will take into the examination with you. Your notes will contribute to the experience and you may notice something important that others may have missed.

Recognising the experience is at the heart of responses to section C and your teacher will encourage you to explore reactions in as much detail as possible in order to develop the evaluative vocabulary that you will need to access the higher level of marks.

AFTER YOU HAVE BEEN – CREATING THE NOTES

The limit for the notes is 1,000 words, but you may be able to create useful and accessible notes that are shorter than this. The purpose of the notes, like the annotation of the text in sections A and B, is to jog the memory and to provide something of the thinking behind the answers. The notes in themselves are not the answers to the questions, and you need to be discerning in what you include in your version of the notes. It may well be that less is more here and the compilation of the notes needs to be structured to allow for individuality. Your teacher will encourage you to make the connections between the experiences you have had as a member of the audience and drawing on your research to say how the play might have been presented in original performance conditions.

The basic approach to theatre evaluation has been detailed in *AS Drama and Theatre Studies*, and it is worth reminding you of what we said in relation to Unit 1. Three questions should be addressed in your notes:

1. What did you see?
2. What did you hear?
3. What did you think about it?

Wrapped up in these three basic questions is an opportunity to explore together the experience and to allow for individual responses too. Compiling your individual set of notes should come from the collective exchange of ideas following the visit. There are no hard-and-fast rules on how the notes must be presented as long as you find them accessible during the examination. The more information there is and the more densely packed it is on to the page, the less useful the notes may be. The thinking behind the word limit is to encourage you towards being selective in the information you include in your notes, therefore making them more useful to you during the examination. The notes are a reminder of the experience and a distillation of key elements of research into the appropriate time period; their purpose therefore is to provide support and to give you the confidence to tackle the chosen question.

A useful set of notes should inform the answer and may look something like this, compiled under the following headings:

WORKED EXAMPLE

Live performance seen:

Date:
Venue:

- *Actors and acting techniques/style* with specific examples from specific moments in the production.
- *Design elements* – lighting/sound, costume, setting/staging with specific examples from specific moments in the production.
- *Directorial decisions*, as far as they are evident from the performance. Specific examples of moments that contributed to the overall impact of the production.

Historical perspective:

Time period:

- *Actors and acting techniques/style.*
- *Design elements.*
- *Directorial decisions and intended impact on audience.*

From your research, there are essentially the same three questions here that need to be covered in relation to the historical connection.

1. What did they see?
2. What did they hear?
3. What might they have felt about it?

Wrapped up in these three questions is the need to have some research in place that will as far as possible give you an understanding of the performance conditions of the time. This will enable you to make the connection between the experience you have had as part of the course and the experience an audience might have had in the chosen period. The role of the director in the historical context is an interesting one to explore, for example, and will lead to some conclusions being drawn in relation to the live performance seen and its likely original performance conditions.

It is probably a good idea to have two A4 sheets for the notes, taped together side by side. When the notes are opened out on the desk you will have the notes on the live performance on the left and the notes on the historical connections on the right, with the headings reading across both pages to make the link more obvious for access under examination conditions. You may decide to colour-code elements within the notes to make them stand out from the page at a glance and therefore make them more immediate and accessible for you during the examination.

Your notes may be handwritten, or they may be electronically produced, whichever you feel more comfortable with. There are only two rules about this. One is around the word limit. Some of you will be able to have sufficient information to help support your answers in less than 1,000 words, others will go up to the limit. Sketches and diagrams are useful and, where appropriate, these may form the basis of versions that could be dropped into the answer. As long as the purpose is clear and there is annotation to inform the examiner, a well-placed sketch or diagram could be supportive of a point made in response to the question. Drawings, diagrams or sketches in themselves will probably not enable you to access the higher level of marks but a well-annotated sketch that is explored in the body of the answer and illustrates a particular point for clarification purposes may be just what the examiner is looking for.

The other rule is that there should be no pre-produced material included in the notes – for example, photographs or extracts from the programme. This does not mean that the programme is not a useful tool in preparing for this unit as there are many useful programmes being produced by theatres that will often place the production in its historical context and give useful background to the play and playwright. You do not need to all buy a programme, although it is often useful to have one to keep as you may wish to start to build up your theatre-going history for future reference. The programme information needs to be discussed, weighed up and its relative merit assessed against the word limit for notes. Deciding what might be relevant needs to be seen in relation to the kinds of questions that might be asked in this section. Just because it is included in the programme does not mean that it is automatically useful to you in the examination.

Your teacher will probably guide you here towards creating sets of notes that will be effective for you in the examination room. It may be that everybody in your teaching group will compile their notes in exactly the same way and there is nothing to say that you should not do this. It may be the case, though, that different students will be able to access information in different ways and this diversity of approach should also be encouraged, as long as the information does not exceed the overall word limit. The source material for most of you will be exactly the same:

- The live performance seen as a member of the audience.
- The historical period related to the live performance seen.

The response to the live performance will be a collective one, from which individual sets of notes will be compiled to take into the examination.

THE EXAMINER AND YOU

There is a choice of two questions in this section, one of which will always start with a quotation to stimulate thinking and to elicit a response. The quotation or statement will usually be provocative and challenge your thinking about the way theatre could be seen now in relation to how it may have been seen in its original performance conditions. If you are going to answer this question – and there is nothing to say that you should not – you must always keep an eye on the statement in order to be able to access the top bands of marks, as it is this which will help the examiner to assess your level of understanding of the performance seen. It is not enough for you to write that you do not agree with the statement and then present a prepared answer lifted directly from your notes. The whole of your response should be peppered with examples of why you do not agree with the statement, supported by reasons from your understanding of the performance seen live and its historical context. You may agree or disagree with the statement and the examiner will be looking for either response, but the argument that will develop within the answer should be very clear and structured in a way that enables the examiner, who may not have seen the particular production, to understand why it is that you have chosen to respond in the way you have. The statement itself may get you going and you may find that you strongly disagree with it, but, in a cool and measured way, you need to look at it in relation to the production you have seen and decide whether or not there is enough material in that production to enable you to give a good response.

You need to remember that the examiner is neutral when it comes to the response itself except to assess how far it engages with the question, and whether you are able to offer support for your standpoint from a position of knowledge. There is no point any student setting out to 'please the examiner' with an overly effusive answer because this is what the student thinks the examiner will expect.

> *The Examiner says:*
>
> **It is true, that, at this level of study your examiner might expect that all students will be able to recognise the theatrical achievements within a performance even if the performance itself is not to your liking. The question in Unit 4 is not about to what extent you have liked the production or, indeed, the chosen text for sections A and B, but to what extent you have recognised and appreciated the elements that have gone into making it what it is today, seen against the elements that made it what it was in its original performance conditions. It is not therefore your research that is important in this question, but your understanding and application of the information you have gleaned.**

The other question in this section will tend to focus on a specific aspect of the production and asks you to explore this aspect to demonstrate an understanding of what you saw in relation to what might have been. The focus may be on acting techniques, design elements or directorial decisions – or a combination of these elements. You need to be aware that the focus of the question and your ability to recognise this in the response will form the major part of the examiner's assessment of your work. As we have already indicated in relation to section B, the 'scattergun' approach to this section will prove to be just as unsuccessful. Your response must be focused in relation to the question if you are to access the higher marks.

The questions in this section are generic but the response must be specific. The questions are structured to enable you to write about a production of a play from any one of the three possible time periods for this section. Your teacher will probably want to explore with you the questions and the assessment criteria, as the focus of the question is often more specific than it at first appears. Do not be taken in by initial appearances; this is A level work and demands a response from you to reflect this.

Like section A and section B, this section is not about the play but about the production of the play, and the examiner will ignore passages in the answer that are not relevant, however interesting they may be. You may feel that it is important to demonstrate your knowledge of a wide range of concepts and ideas in relation to the theatrical experience that you think may be of interest to your examiner. It is not a good idea to do so as you are, in effect, self-penalising, taking up time and space that your coherent answer to the question that has been set should be occupying. A question about actors, for example, is not a character study but it is asking you to demonstrate an understanding of how actors used specific techniques in order to portray their role to the audience within this particular production of the play. The response may include some reference to the character at a specific moment and this may be necessary to support the observation about the actor's technique, but it must be this way around, not the actor mentioned almost in passing in a response that focuses heavily on the text rather than on the performance. The following extract from a response to a production of *A Midsummer Night's Dream* gives some idea of the balance in a response where it is clearly acting skills that are at the heart of the response but an understanding of the character is also evident, giving a confident response that is balanced towards the performance, not the text. The response also heads towards the connection with the original performance conditions by linking the same moment and the same characters with the moment and the characters in the original. This is probably a good way of connecting the now and the then of the performance.

WORKED EXAMPLE

The thrust stage created a strong actor-audience relationship. I felt I was observing events but it wasn't as if they were just acting it on a stage. I suspended my disbelief and engaged fully with the action on stage through the depth of the emotion (e.g. between Oberon (Dixon) and Titania (Harris)) through pauses, facial expression and the acknowledgement of the audience, for example when the lovers were all on stage chasing each other, and Walter (Helena) broke the moment, turned to the audience and pulled a sarcastic facial expression. Even though I was pulled out of moments at times, it was still engaging to watch in that it made me laugh, feel sympathy for Helena (Walter) while she was pursuing her love Demetrius and also Hermia (Drysdale) when Lysander (Davey) turned affections to Helena. Whether the same moment in its original performance conditions would have been as comical for the same reasons is difficult to say. What we do know though is that all of the actors would have been male and the audience would have needed to suspend their disbelief in the same away as I did in order to accept the relationships that were being presented to them at this moment in the play.

The examiner would look for each of the points covered in these 18 lines to be expanded and developed with some specifics in place in order to be able to assess the level of understanding demonstrated. It is a good start and there is enough here to let the examiner know that this student has an understanding of what has been seen and how this might connect into the historical context of the play. The development of the general statements made here with the specifics will now be very important.

19 The historical periods

MAKING THE HISTORICAL CONNECTIONS IN UNIT 4

There are three major periods of theatrical development that you need to be aware of for Unit 4, two of which will have more impact on your work than the third. Once you know which text you are exploring for sections A and B, this will indicate the choice of time periods for the play you see in performance for section C.

The three major periods are:

- 525 BC–AD 65
- 1564–1720
- 1828–1914.

In sections A and B, the play you will explore will have been written and originally performed in one of these three time periods and in section C you will respond to a live production you see of a play written and originally performed in one of the other two time periods.

525 BC–AD 65

You should consider:

- The place of theatre in the society of the time.
- Its impact on each section of society.
- The conventions of the theatre space of the time.
- The conventions of performance.
- The intended impact on the audience.
- The specifics of Old Comedy and the work of Aristophanes (for sections A and B).

1564–1720

You should consider:

- The place of theatre in the society of the time.
- Its impact on each section of society.
- The conventions of the theatre space of the time.
- The conventions of performance.
- The intended impact on the audience.
- The specifics of the work of Christopher Marlowe (for sections A and B).

1828–1914

You should consider:

- The place of theatre in the society of the time.
- Its impact on each section of society.
- The conventions of the theatre space of the time.
- The conventions of performance.
- The intended impact on the audience.
- The specifics of the work of Georg Buchner (for sections A and B).

Across the unit, the examiner is looking for you to be able to demonstrate an understanding of the social, cultural and historical context of the play. Very simply this is connecting the now and then of the experience and trying to identify what it is about the play in performance that still makes it relevent for a twenty-first-century audience.

Your research should help you make the connections and should give you information that may be relevent in your interpretation for section B, such as the state of war that Athens was in at the time Aristophanes wrote *Lysistrata*. It was as much an anti-war play of its day as it is now, using the broad humour of Old Comedy to highlight the plight of women losing loved ones in a pointless conflict.

If you consider the live performance you see for section C to be defined as:

- what did you see;
- what did you hear;
- what did you think about it,

you could consider the historical connection as follows:

- what might they have seen;
- what might they have heard;
- what might they have thought about it?

With this simple structure in mind you are already thinking in terms of making clear and obvious connections between the 'now' and the 'then' of the experience in the play's history for section C, and this same process might be just as useful for preparing the chosen text for section A and section B. The whole unit is about making connections and making reference to the historical perspective in order to demonstrate how you might be able to bring your understanding to bear on the theatre of the twenty-first century, recognising the elements of theatre there may be in place in order to have an impact on the audience.

The starting point of all of your responses is you and your experience, but this must indicate an understanding of the material and where it has come from. You cannot be general about this, you do need to have done the research and you do need to be able to demonstrate this in your answers.

Extension Activity

Exploring the historical perspective

Consider the evaluation by a student of a production of *Romeo and Juliet* that follows. Read the evaluation and then read it again with the following question in mind:

Evaluate the influence of the director on the theatre of the twenty-first century by comparing the production you have seen to its original performance conditions. All references to its original performance conditions have been removed from this response. Using your research material and the question above, write what you might consider to be appropriate references to the original performance conditions that could go into the response where indicated.

Before going to see Michael Bogdanov's *Romeo and Juliet*, I researched the director to get an understanding of the style of directing he used and to get an idea of how the play might be laid out. According to reviews, Michael Bogdanov attempts to modernise *Romeo and Juliet* and to therefore have a major impact on the production *(insert historical reference)*.

I read reviews of this production prior to seeing it and was given an impression of a balanced amount of criticism and praise for his production. I was slightly disappointed with the performance; I felt that the actors could have put more energy and emotion into their characters. I also felt that the performance was let down by using comedy at serious points in the play such as the Mercrutio/Tybalt fight scene *(insert historical reference)*. I was also disappointed with the ending of the production, because after Juliet (Sara Lloyd-Gregory) kills herself there is a blackout, then a gold statue appeared centre stage, Lord Capulet and Lord Montague entered from stage right and stage left respectively, then suddenly a barrage of news reporters, journalists and photographers arrived, taking pictures and talking to cameramen as if doing a live broadcast, and interviewing key characters, then Lord Montague and Lord Capulet shook hands and posed for a picture in front of the statue. I felt that this ending was an anti-climax but clearly part of the director's influence on the production *(insert historical reference)*.

I think the biggest disappointment was the lack of emotion in Jack Ryder's portrayal of Romeo; an example of this is when he visits Juliet's tomb and discovers her dead, but he didn't appear distraught; he was sad but not distraught. I felt that Jack Ryder could have invested more time working on his character; his portrayal lacked depth of character in this central role *(insert historical reference)*.

The stage was set within a Proscenium arch. The Proscenium arch creates a 'window frame' around the scenery and actors. The advantage is that it gives everyone in the audience a good view because the actors need only focus on one direction rather than continually moving around the stage to give a good view from all sides. A proscenium arch stage also simplifies the hiding and obscuring of objects from the audience's view (sets, actors not currently performing and theatre technology) *(insert historical reference)*.

Bogdanov's idea was to create a more modern version of *Romeo and Juliet*. One prop that showed this was guns, which made the play modern because swords were used in the original version. Another prop used was knives, possibly to highlight the amount of knife crime in this day and age *(insert historical reference)*.

I think what the Designer Sean Crowley had in mind was to modernise the costume by dressing the actors in contemporary clothes. I rather liked the costumes because they helped show which house a particular character was from. For example, the Capulets wore leather jackets and more formal clothing whereas the Montagues opted for a more laid-back style of clothing, such as T-shirts, shorts, hats and a more modern style of clothing. I think the clothes worn by the two families contrasted with each other. The Capulets wore dark clothes such as suits and leather, while the Montagues wore bright T-shirts and baggy trousers in a wide variety of different colours *(insert historical reference)*.

Another way the director had an influence on the production was by modernising how the characters moved. A good example of this was that the

Capulets seemed to swagger while the Montagues walked in a relaxed, carefree way, enhancing their physicality. I also noticed a contrast in vehicles used by the two families. For example, the Capulets had a motorbike which is seen as a fast powerful machine, like its owner Tybalt, and the Montagues had a moped which may be seen as a casual, slow and calm vehicle, similar to its owner Benvolio. I found that this greatly enhanced the dynamics and energised the scenes *(insert historical reference)*.

The way they talked however remained unchanged; they spoke in Shakespearean grammar and kept to the original script as far as I could tell, using an even tone of voice. One example of modernisation is when Benvolio arrived on stage on his moped; I think this grabbed the attention of the audience effectively, because it was not something they expected *(insert historical reference)*.

The stage had a chequered floor; the squares were black and white like a chess board which usually has two teams, and this staging may symbolise yin and yang, light and dark, Capulet and Montague (*insert historical reference*).

It had a projected backdrop of scenes of Verona. This made the stage seem bigger and gave the impression that the play took place outside. In the scene after the Capulet party, Jack Ryder (Romeo) had gone to see Sara Lloyd-Gregory (Juliet) in her garden while she was thinking about Romeo and why she could not be with Romeo because of their families. In this scene dark blue colours are used for the lighting with some white showing night, but the colours also set the mood of the scene and in this scene the blue lighting was used to show romance. The romance between Romeo and Juliet was a dark secret from their parents and the darkness was associated with this scene *(insert historical reference)*.

The director's influence on the lighting was also seen at the party which was very modern, using disco lights and strobe effects to make the this scene more realistic for a twenty-first-century audience. The use of these lights makes the scene more energetic and gives off the party mood. It also makes the scene more modern, because they would not have been able to use lighting effects in the original period of history *(insert historical reference)*.

The sounds used were also very modern, and were also used to show where the sene is set, such as outside, where there was the sound of a chattering crowd. I think this gave the effect that the scene was set outside with a lot of people milling around. Music was also used during the disco scene; a variety of pop, dance and techno was used for the scene *(insert historical reference)*.

To conclude, I think that the director of the theatre in the twenty-first century has a major impact on a production and is able to call on a range of experts in his company to give him – or her – the effects he is looking for. This was certainly not the case when the play was originally performed, as there was no director as we know it, and the performance relied very much on the actors engaging with their audience.

Knowing the historical perspective is about being able to make the connections as well as being aware of what went on and why. From Ancient Greece to Elizabethan England and nineteenth-century Germany, the relationship between theatre and its society is clearly defined. In order to access the full range of marks in Unit 4 you will need to be able to selectively define your understanding of the connections you make.

20 Theatre evaluation

EVALUATING LIVE THEATRE IN SECTION C IN RELATION TO THE QUESTIONS

As we have already established, section C is a response to a live performance of a play written and originally performed in one of the following three time periods:

- 525 BC – AD 65
- 1564 – 1720
- 1828 – 1914.

We need to go into this in a little more detail now in order for you to be clear about what this section is demanding of you. The live performance should be seen as your primary source of information for this section and it should help you to form the structure for your answer, as everything you write about in response to the section C question starts with your response to the live performance.

If your primary source is the performance you see live, then your secondary source is the original performance conditions of the play. You have a choice of two questions in this section and you must choose one question to answer. You need to be careful to look at the demands of the question in relation to the information you have on the secondary source before you start to answer it.

What is the question asking you? There is information in the question that will ask you to focus your response and you will need to look for this information before you start to answer it. A question will not ask you to write down everything you know about the performance but, like the other questions in this unit, it will focus your response so that you can demonstrate your understanding of the live production in relation to its original performance conditions.

Your teacher may have some examples of questions that he or she may have been working through with you. Have a look at the pairs of questions that follow, as these represent the kinds of questions that you are likely to come across in section C.

Pair 1

'Theatre is a product of its time but its themes and issues are timeless.'

Discuss the play you have seen in performance in the light of this statement and with reference to its original performance conditions.

Or

Evaluate the influence of the director on the theatre of the twenty-first century by comparing the production you have seen with its original performance conditions.

Pair 2

'Theatre in the twenty-first century is full of tricks and gimmicks.'

Comment on the play you have seen in production in the light of this statement and by reference to its original performance conditions.

Or

Discuss the way ideas were communicated to the audience in the production you saw, comparing it to its original performance conditions.

Pair 3

'Theatre should be about the way we live now, not the way we used to live.'

Discuss this statement in the light of the play you have seen in performance to show your understanding of how you think the impact of the play has altered since its original performance.

Or

Referring to the production you have seen, discuss how an audience might have reacted to this staging of the play in its original performance conditions.

Look carefully at the three pairs of questions and note the similarities and the differences.

Note the following:

- Each question has the live performance as its starting point and this should remind you of your approach to the response.
- One question in each pair starts with a quotation for you to consider in your response. This is the pattern for this unit.
- All questions are about performance, not about play. This is important for you to think about in your answer, in which you should consider:
  - What did I see?
  - What did I hear?
  - What did I think about it?

In this unit you have two pieces of information to support your responses to the questions:

1. Your annotated copy of the text explored for section A and section B.
2. Research notes on the play in performance, connecting it to its original performance conditions.

We will go into some detail on the research notes as they will form the basis for your response to the question. It may be worth going back to your AS experience at this point and looking again at the evaluation notes you prepared following the theatre visit for Unit 1. We offer some thoughts on evaluating live theatre, in some detail, in AS *Drama and Theatre Studies*, and you could use this as a starting point too. The initial reaction you will have to the live performance is exactly the same as your evaluation in Unit 1 but, because this is now A level work you need to have information to connect your evaluation with the original performance conditions of the play.

THE RESEARCH NOTES

This work needs to contain information to support your response to section C – it is not the answer to the question, it is your thinking behind the answer. Your research notes need to be divided into two sections – one for the primary source and one for the secondary source you will have researched. The primary source is the live performance and the secondary source is its original performance conditions. The amount of information you have in your notes is limited to up to 1,000 words and, of course, by the time you will have in the examination to refer to them.

Your approach should be that too much is as unhelpful as too little. What you could do to help you compile your notes is to try setting out both sections each on an A4 sheet of paper and taping the two sheets of paper together. The sheet on the left should always be the primary source, as this should always be the starting point for your response. To the right as you look at it is the secondary source, the original performance conditions.

The more performance based your research notes are, the more useful they will be to you, as the question is about performance and your answer needs to reflect this. If you divide your notes up into the following headings under your primary source, you can then map across to the secondary source sheet with corresponding evidence from your research.

Possible headings:

- Acting
- Design
- Director
- Overall impressions

COMPILING YOUR RESEARCH NOTES

Compiling your research notes should be a group activity and should involve gaining an understanding, not just gathering information.

Divide your group into pairs and allocate an aspect of the original time period to each pair – depending on how many of you there are in the group. Set a time for reporting back and stick to it. Use the reporting back session as an opportunity to ask questions and to make sure that the information you have in your notes is relevant and therefore of use to you. There is no time in the examination for sifting through pages of extraneous material and it is very frustrating knowing the information is there but not being able to find it because of the way you have compiled your notes. Your research needs to be into the social, cultural and historical context of the play in relation to its original performance conditions. You will all see the primary source performance, so you should all share in compiling the notes for that performance.

Good research notes will be helpful to you in the examination and, within the 1,000 words maximum that you are allowed, it could therefore mean that less is more. The figure given is a maximum and it could be that you are able to compile your notes in 500 words, and these may be just as helpful to you as a set of notes that goes up to the maximum word count. If you revisit

Unit 1, your Theatre Evaluation had to be up to a maximum of 1,000 words too, so that will give you some idea of how the word limit may work for you. The difference between now and then is that these notes need to include information on the original performance conditions as well.

What your notes might cover

The following areas should be covered as a minimum in the evaluation following the live theatre visit. Some of the information that you compile collectively will then form the basis for your notes on your primary source:

- Title, venue, date.
- Names of principal actors, designer(s) and director.
- First impressions before the performance starts.
- The impact of the first five minutes – how was it achieved?
- Theatrical devices evident in the performance – specific examples.
- Acting techniques evident in the performance – specific examples.
- How did the production engage you as a member of the audience?
- Was your reaction the same as the reaction of those around you – as far as you could tell?
- General and specific observations on the look and feel of the production – costume, set and staging, lighting, specific lighting effects.
- General and specific observations on the aural elements of the performance – delivery of dialogue, sound effects (live/recorded), music (live/recorded).
- What did you feel about the performance and the impact it made on you as a student of drama?

Remember: when you go to the theatre, you have a job to do. You are an active participant not a passive observer.

Your notes on your secondary source should then follow the same pattern, reflecting as far as possible your understanding of the live production you have seen and how this may have compared to its original performance conditions. Now you have the notes in place, you need to consider how to use them in the examination room.

Notes are useful only if you can access them easily and understand them. These are your notes, and the format and structure are in your hands, as you are the person who is going to have to access them in the examination room. You may be guided by your teacher or by what we have written here but, ultimately, you need to be able to find nuggets of information to drop where appropriate into your responses. There is little point in having too much information in your notes, or too much annotation in your copy of the text for section A and section B, as you will not have the opportunity to read through a lot of information in order to drop it into your answer. Bullet points and/or some form of colour coding is probably the easiest way of making your notes accessible for you.

Section C is about evaluation, it is not about reporting the experience. You need to have an opinion that you are able to express based on your experience as a member of the audience and as a student of drama who has accessed appropriate research that has shaped your opinion of what you have experienced in the light of your understanding of what the audience might have experienced during the original performance.

21 Deconstructing the questions

Unit 4 is made up of two essay-type questions and one question that is subdivided into three parts, each of which is worth a different mark. In this chapter, we will look at the questions in some detail and explore the language used within the given structure. The chapter is primarily about the way the Exam Board uses words in relation to the assessment criteria, but it is also about how you might structure your response to questions once you have a more clear understanding of what is actually being demanded of you.

There is not a question on the exam paper that will simply ask you to tell the examiner everything you know about the chosen text or everything you have understood from the play you have seen in performance. The question is designed to encourage you to be focused in your answer, not to give as much information as you can in the allotted time and space. You need to consider this carefully in relation to the wording of the questions.

No matter what words are contained there, the most important thing you can do in all of your answers is to justify everything you are saying in theatrical terms. It is not enough to describe what you would hope to achieve in section A and section B or to list what you recognise in the performance you write about in section C; your answer must contain reasons to support your observations. As a general rule of thumb, the following structure applies to your responses:

- *this is what I think*
- *this is why I think it*
- *this is an example to support my thinking.*

This approach will generally give you the structure in your work that will enable you to access the top bands of marks providing, of course, that what you are writing is relevant to the question that has been set.

You need to look at the wording in the question carefully. It might be a good idea to underline what you consider to be the key words in each question and what the focus should therefore be in your response. Consider the following question, write it out in your notebook and underline or highlight what you think are the key words in it:

As a director, outline how you would approach a production of your chosen play for a specific audience of your choice.

KEY WORDS

The clues to your response are in the question itself. You might therefore underline or highlight the following words:

- director
- production
- specific audience

Consider the following question and carry out the same exercise:

Outline your approach to rehearsing this extract in order to bring out its essential impact on your audience.

KEY WORDS

In this case you might underline or highlight the following words:

- rehearsing
- essential impact
- audience

Once you are into the routine of preparing your responses in this way it will become almost second nature to highlight or underline the key words in the question which will help you to target your response and give a visual reminder as you work through the question of what it is you should be including in your answer. What should be reassuring is that there should be no words in the question that are unfamiliar to you.

Conclusion: drawing the course together

This chapter will bring the A2 year, and the course, to a close by both reflecting on some of the experiences we have had so far, and by specifically looking to the A2 year and Units 3 and 4 in the context of the course as a whole and experiences you will have had that may be useful when looking at UCAS applications, for example. Part of reflecting on what you have been involved in is to put your thoughts in order and to start to build up a picture of your experiences that is much more specific than being able to say: '*I did drama and theatre studies at A level. It was great.*'

You will be doing some planning towards what you hope to be involved in post-18 at an early stage in the A2 year and those of you who are applying to drama schools will have auditions, probably in the spring term. Almost without exception you will be making applications somewhere and most of you will be considering higher education.

There is always a fine line between underselling yourself and over-confidence in your achievements and your assessment of your achievements. Tutors are usually very good at reigning in enthusiasms or encouraging revelations. What a tutor is not always so clear about is the experience you have had as a student of drama and theatre studies, and the complexities of the learning that has taken place during this course.

From September of the A2 year you have been challenged with creating approaches to performance that are fitting for this level of study. There is no doubt that the A2 year has stretched your understanding of how drama and theatre works, but, perhaps more importantly, it has tested your developmental skills as a deviser and as a director. The AS year was about exploring and responding and gathering the tools of your trade in order to unleash yourself upon the demands of devising and directing that form the basic structure of the A2 year.

Looking back on the demands of the A2 year, you can clearly see the structure that put your experiences into the context of the assessment criteria. Unit 3 was about creating an original piece of theatre from a given source and Unit 4 was about you responding to a given text and theatrical time period from the position of a director and as an informed member of a theatre audience.

Your experience in Unit 3 may have led you to devise performances with a specific audience in mind, creating theatre to a brief either from your teacher or from another body or organisation; for example, a local primary school looking for work on road safety or stranger danger for Years 5 and 6. You may have been set the task of researching and presenting a piece of work on a given theme or arising from a stimulus in the style of a practitioner other than any you may have looked at specifically as part of the course in the AS year. You may have been given a play text as a starting point for Unit 3 and your task could have been to deconstruct it in order to create a new performance piece that highlights a theme or idea from the original.

Whatever your approach to Unit 3, you have made a valuable contribution as a member of that devising company and you have demonstrated a range of skills in order to be able to access the marks for the unit. You will have learned a great deal about yourself and the people with whom you have worked.

You will have needed to do some historical research in order to access the questions in Unit 4. Your teacher may have set a project for you to research one of the given time periods for Unit 4 and given you a time limit, after which you had to present your findings to the rest of your group. Your teacher may have set this task for you in twos or threes, depending on the total numbers in your class, but you will have needed to make decisions about what material you thought was relevant and how to present the results of your research to your fellow students in the most accessible way possible. You will have listened to presentations from others too, and needed to make notes that you considered the most helpful to you in the examination, formatting them in such a way as to make them succinct and easily accessible under examination conditions.

We are setting out for you here what you might have done in order to access the A2 units and you may have just automatically got on with it without really thinking about what was involved and the learning you were involved in. You will probably have done some background reading and preparing extracts for performance. With Unit 4 in mind, your teacher may have set you extracts from the text you studied for Unit 4 with the aim of helping you to be more familiar with the text and to have a better understanding of the performance demands you faced when looking at the text to help you prepare for the final unit of the course. You may have been encouraged to prepare and deliver a workshop around the chosen text as a director working in the rehearsal room and you will have needed to structure the rehearsal to help both you and your fellow students further your knowledge of the text and of rehearsal techniques that might be used to explore it.

You will have been on at least one theatre visit in the A2 year. Some schools and colleges are fortunate enough to be able to arrange two- or three-day trips to see a variety of performances in order to help students gain a better understanding of how directors will approach a range of texts in order to bring them to life for an audience. You will have seen a production with section C of Unit 4 in mind but you may also have seen others too.

You may have looked at some of the extension activities in this book and spent some time exploring them on your own or with fellow students. This approach to independence is a skill in itself that you need to recognise when you are preparing your personal statement and CV for the future.

You will not have been able to move on from AS to A2 without a period of reflection, and some of that will inevitably have happened once your results for the AS year were available. We hope that you achieved the UMS points you were looking for in order to encourage you to go on to the A2 year with a realistic final grade in mind. Your teacher will have become more of a guiding figure in the A2 year, giving you opportunities to use the skills you developed during the AS year in order for you to be able to access the criteria for assessment in the second year.

There will have been teaching that will have enabled your learning to take place but a lot of the decisions you will have made will have been your decisions, rather than those put forward by your teacher. You needed confidence that you were able to work in a more guided structure than in a heavily directed one. Before you close this book, take another look around you. Those people sitting with you supported you in hopefully getting the grade you wanted from this course, and you will have done the same for them. Do not underestimate what you have achieved. Whatever the final result, whatever the grade you achieve, you will have been part of one of the most complex creative experiences of any group of students working at this level of study. Whatever else you may do in the future, do not sell yourself short as a student of A level Drama and Theatre Studies.

Appendix 1
Drama school or drama degree?

THE DIFFERENCES AND HOW YOU GO ABOUT STUDYING DRAMA POST-18

A DRAMA DEGREE

There is a huge range of drama-related courses that you can study at university but these are very different to learning the skill of becoming an actor. While many university courses have some practical elements to them, they are essentially an extension of your Drama and Theatre Studies A level course, so they will also look at theory and involve some written elements. To study drama at university means just that; you are learning more about drama as a subject in its own right.

A straight drama or Drama and Theatre Studies degree tends to be more prestigious than a Performing Arts-type course and the grades they ask for are correspondently more demanding. For example, to study for a BA in Drama at Royal Holloway, which is part of the University of London, the current standard requirement for conditional offers is ABB. They are very clear that while their course offers a superb range of options, it does not in its own right equip you to be an actor. It is likely that you would have to go on to do postgraduate training at a drama school if this is what you ultimately wished to do. While it is demanding to get into university to study drama, the route is clear and possible, and most enthusiastic, suitable candidates who get the grades gain a place. If you have struggled with the A level course, however, then perhaps this route is not for you.

DRAMA SCHOOL

Drama schools are very different to universities, although most do offer a degree qualification – a BA in Acting. This training is full-time and consists of about eight hours a day for at least five days a week. You will find that this is often extended to late evenings and weekends. While you may look at the course and think that there appear to be a great deal of demands placed on you compared to other students following other courses, the reality is that it is even more intensive and demanding than it at first appears. Despite this, competition for places is fierce; it is not unusual for 3,000 students to apply for 30 places.

You cannot apply to drama school from a standing start. They will probably ask for two GCE A levels or their equivalent, but their main criteria are looking to you to demonstrate your potential and that you are suitable to be trained as an actor. Applying to drama school should not be a sudden whim. You need to have been preparing for this almost from the moment you took your first steps.

Students who can demonstrate a genuine interest in drama and theatre put themselves ahead of the crowd. It is not enough to express a passion, you need to have lived it too. Many schools will ask about your performance experience, which is why it is a great start to have done other production work outside school or college. Youth theatres are ideal for this and many drama school applicants are also in the National Youth Theatre (http://www.nyt.org.uk/).

The best way to check out the 22 UK drama schools is to go on the website, which links them altogether. They belong to a group known as The Conference of Drama Schools (http://www.drama.ac.uk/). Every autumn, they produce a useful little book which is a guide to the 22 schools and the courses they offer. It details how you apply and you can link to each individual institution through the website, giving you the opportunity to explore the courses and surroundings in more depth.

You will see from the websites that some of the recognised schools have to be applied for through UCAS, while others have their own application process. This could give you numerous chances of gaining a place. You could, for example, apply to five schools through UCAS and perhaps another five outside of UCAS. The process is expensive however. At the time of writing the average cost of an audition fee is £40, so if you applied to ten schools this would cost £400. The hidden costs come in travelling to the audition and, unless you live in London and are applying only to London schools, you can factor in £100 for each drama school applied to, to include the audition fee, travel and expenses for the day. We think it is realistic to say: be prepared to be disappointed! You have to have a strong and well-balanced personality to handle rejection as often as actors do, and applying to drama school is the first step of the process. Many schools test your resilience by rejecting you the first time you apply, most prefer slightly older students and certainly uptake is more common in subsequent attempts at applying.

Simon Dunmore has written a useful book called *An Actor's Guide to Getting Work* published by A & C Black (London 2007) and it starts with the process of getting into drama school.

Appendix 2
Useful websites

Look out for updates on our own website which supports and expands on our ideas in the two books that support the A level course.

www.actorsofdionysus.com: AOD is a company committed to producing high-quality work, pushing back the boundaries while exploring, mainly, the classics – hence the name – but not exclusively.

www.bigbrum.org.uk: Big Brum TIE has been working in Birmingham and the West Midlands since 1982. The company tours throughout the region to schools and colleges, working with pupils and students across the full age range. Big Brum tours two TIE programmes a year (one in the autumn term, and the other in the spring and summer terms) and offers other more specific projects to the education sector.

www.bruvvers.co.uk: The North East's foremost touring company. Bruvvers have been taking popular theatre to the community for more than 35 years. They are based in Newcastle upon Tyne, giving approximately 250 performances per year and playing to more than 40,000 people. They are an ensemble company with at least three plays in repertoire at any one time. Their shows are exciting and original and are aimed at all the family; they also help with workshops, festivals, conferences, teaching, enabling and passing on skills to all age ranges.

www.complicite.org: The website of the leading physical theatre company, giving news and updates on current and past productions. This constantly evolving ensemble of performers and collaborators has made an important impact on theatre for over 20 years.

www.donmarwarehouse.com: The Donmar Warehouse is a 250-seat subsidised theatre located in the heart of London's West End, close to Covent Garden with a reputation as one of the UK's leading producing theatres. It has an excellent reputation with many actors queuing up to work in its intimate, challenging space. As well as presenting at least six productions a year at its home in Covent Garden, the Donmar presents work nationally and internationally.

www.DV8.co.uk: DV8 Physical Theatre was formed in 1986 and is led by Lloyd Newson. To date,the company has produced 15 highly acclaimed dance pieces, which have toured internationally, and five award-winning films for television. Exciting, challenging and, to some, controversial work that pushes back the boundaries in style, form and content.

www.edexcel.org.uk: The website of the Examination Board, constantly updated and a source of very useful information in relation to the range of qualifications on offer.

www.franticassembly.co.uk: Since its formation in 1994 Frantic assembly has toured extensively throughout the UK and abroad, building its reputation as one of the country's most exciting companies. Producing thrilling, energetic and uncompromising theatre, the company creates theatre that reflects contemporary culture and attracts wide audiences.

www.guardian.co.uk: The home of the newspaper and great for online updates of what is going on in the world around you – including excellent coverage of the Arts.

www.hulltruck.co.uk: Established in 1971, Hull Truck is one of only six producing theatres in the Yorkshire region, and has been offering a range of performances and workshops from its base in Hull since 1983. Throughout its history, Hull Truck has continued to push artistic boundaries as a pioneering force of contemporary British theatre. Arguably, the company is most famous for John Godber and *Bouncers*.

www.kaostheatre.com: The home of Kaos Theatre Company under the artistic direction of Xavier Levet. Always worth a visit and Kaos will thrill, surprise and shock, often in equal measure. This is what theatre is all about.

www.kneehigh.co.uk: From its home in Cornwall, Kneehigh Theatre has built a reputation for creating vigorous and popular theatre for audiences throughout the UK and beyond. In Cornwall, Kneehigh created theatre for families in locations within their communities and, from these simple beginnings, the company now finds itself celebrated as one of Britain's most exciting touring theatre companies. They create vigorous, popular theatre for a broad spectrum of audiences, using a multi-talented group of performers. A spontaneous sense of risk and adventure produces extraordinary dramatic results. Themes explored by Kneehigh are universal and local, epic and domestic, with recent acclaimed productions as diverse as *Brief Encounter*, *Tristen and Isolde* and *A Matter of Life and Death*.

www.laban.org: The website of the company that explores all the possibilities of contemporary dance and gives information about courses, classes, jobs and news, including details of forthcoming related auditions.

www.nationaltheatre.org.uk: The National Theatre in London. A powerhouse of performance, incorporating an exciting mix of productions of classic and contemporary pieces. Well worth a visit in its own right with organised tours and talkback sessions offered on a regular basis. The good thing is that it is not as expensive as you might think!

www.northern-broadsides.co.uk: Formed in 1992 by Artistic Director Barrie Rutter, Northern Broadsides is a multi-award-winning touring company based in Halifax, West Yorkshire. The company has built up an excellent reputation performing Shakespeare and classical texts with an innovative, popular and regional style. It could be said that Northern Broadsides' work is characterised by its vitality and humour; the passion of the performers; a refreshing ensemble style which adds tangible coherence to the performances, and precise direction which results in work of great clarity and simplicity.

www.nyt.org.uk: If you are aged between 13 and 21, the National Youth Theatre, Britain's première youth theatre company, is just the place for you! Look out for audition information that is sent into schools and colleges on a regular basis and visit the website for up-to-date information on forthcoming projects. The NYT performed at the handover ceremony following the 2008 Olympics.

www.officiallondontheatre.co.uk: A great way of keeping up with what is happening on the London stage with news, reviews, updates and offers. It is worth dipping into this site on a regular basis.

www.rsc.org.uk: The website of the Royal Shakespeare Company that is informative on a whole range of topics, including production news, interviews and regular updates on what is happening in the company.

www.royalcourttheatre.com: The Royal Court is a world leader in theatre, producing new plays of the highest quality, encouraging new writers, and challenging the nature of theatre of our time. Dedicated to new work by innovative writers from the UK and around the world, the theatre's pivotal role in promoting new voices is undisputed. From *Bond* to *Churchill* to *Kane* and *Ravenhill*, The Royal Court continues to excite and surprise its audiences.

www.samuelfrench-london.co.uk: If it is in print, it is probably available from Samuel French, world renowned for publishing acting editions of play scripts.

www.shakespeares-globe.org: The site dedicated to the Globe Theatre and keeping you updated with production news, tour details and special offers. A very informative site, particularly when looking at Shakespeare's theatre and performance conditions.

www.stevenberkoff.com: Berkoff's website. News, updates, reviews and special offers on publications and DVDs. Updated regularly, it presents Berkoff and something about his work and style very effectively.

www.theatreroyal.co.ok: The Theatre Royal, Plymouth comes up here but there are a number of Theatre Royals around the country. Your local theatre will have a site similar to this one, keeping you updated on forthcoming productions.

www.thestage.co.uk: *The Stage* is the trade paper that everybody involved in theatre either reads avidly – or avoids like the plague. It keeps you informed and updated but do not expect reviews to be too critical!

Appendix 3 Further reading and suggested viewing

FURTHER READING

This list is not exhaustive and you can dip in and out of most of these books rather than read them from cover to cover. All of them are great for research and expanding your knowledge of the art of the theatre, not only for the A2 year but also if you are currently preparing for the AS course. A wide selection of material at this stage will serve you well for the future.

New thinking is being explored all the time in publications and sometimes theatre styles go out of fashion very quickly. Look out too for newspaper articles and features on actors, directors or theatre companies – these appear more regularly than you think – for views and opinions on the changing state of theatre. Our website that accompanies this book will also be exploring and reviewing new publications on a regular basis.

Benedetti, Jean (1982) *Stanislavski: An Introduction*, Methuen (revised).
Bentley, Eric (1996) *The Life of the Drama*, Applause.
Berkoff, Steven (2008) *Richard II in New York*, Arima Publishing.
Berry, Cicely (2001) *Text in Action*, Virgin Books.
Billington, Michael (2007) *State of the Nation*, Faber and Faber.
Billington, Michael (2007) *Harold Pinter*, Faber and Faber (revised edn).
Bond, Edward (2000) *Selections from the Notebooks*, Methuen.
Braun, Edward (1982) *The Director and the Stage*, Methuen.
Brook, Peter (2008) *The Empty Space*, Penguin (new edn).
Brook, Peter (1995) *There are no Secrets*, Methuen.
Brook, Peter (1989) *The Shifting Point*, Methuen.
Callow, Simon (1984) *Being an Actor*, Methuen.
Cartledge, Paul (1991) *Aristophanes/Theatre of the Absurd*, Bristol Classical Press.
Esslin, Martin (1987) *The Theatre of the Absurd*, Penguin.
Fuegi, John (1995) *The Life and Times of Bertolt Brecht*, Flamingo.
Gottfried, Martin (2003) *Arthur Miller, A Life*, De Capo Press.
Grotowski, Jerry (1975) *Towards a Poor Theatre*, Methuen.
Hall, Peter (2000) *Exposed by the Mask*, Oberon Books.
Hare, David (1990) *Acting Up*, Faber and Faber.
Hirst, David L. (1985) *Edward Bond*, Macmillan.
Holdsworth, Nadine (2006) *Joan Littlewood*, Routledge.

Leach, Robert (2006) *Theatre Workshop: Joan Littlewood*, University of Essex Press.
MacDowell, Douglas M. (1995) *Aristophanes and Athens: An Introduction*, Oxford University Press.
Merlin, Bella (2007) *The Complete Stanislavsky Toolkit*, NHB.
Miller, Arthur (1987) *Timebends – A Life*, Methuen.
Mitchell, Katie (2009) *The Director's Craft*, Routledge.
Nicholl, Charles (2002) *The Reckoning – The Murder of Christopher Marlowe*, Vintage.
Renault, Mary (1966) *The Mask of Apollo*, Longman.
Riggs, David (2005) *The World of Christopher Marlowe*, Faber and Faber.
Sierz, Aleks (2001) *In-yer-face Theatre*, Faber and Faber.
Smith, Ian (2006) *Pinter in the Theatre*, NHB (new edn).
Stafford-Clark, Max (1989) *Letters to George*, Nick Hern.
Stanislavski (1937) *An Actor Prepares*, Methuen.
Thoss, Michael (1994) *Brecht for Beginners*, Writers and Readers.
Willett, John (1978) *Brecht on Theatre*, Methuen.

SUGGESTED VIEWING

There are a number of films with a theatrical slant to them which give an excellent feel of the period in which they are set. Look out for:

Looking for Richard (Al Pacino, 1996). Pacino researching his role as Richard III, featuring a host of well-known faces. As a 'diary of rehearsal', it gives a real insight into the process.
Shakespeare in Love (John Madden, 1998). A romp through Shakespearean England, giving a vivid picture of London at the time and a version of the theatre of the day.
Stage Beauty (Richard Eyre, 2004). Moving on from *Shakespeare in Love*, the position of the greatest 'female' actor is in doubt when women are allowed to appear on the stage. A sense of the period and the politics of the time is evoked.
The Dresser (Peter Yates, 1983). Based on a stage play, the story of an actor manager and his dresser as they cross the country to present the great works in provincial theatres. An evocation of the time and the changing theatrical styles.

There are also numerous versions of well-known plays available – either as filmed versions of the stage production or as film interpretations. Some are more useful than others, but all will provide some insight into the play itself and/or the time period in which it is set and filmed. Again, this list is not exhaustive but there is a real range of experiences here, all of which are available on DVD at the time of writing. Look out for:

A Day in the Death of Joe Egg (Peter Medak, 1972 or Robin Lough, 2002 – TV). A film version of Peter Nicholl's play about a couple coping with life with a severely handicapped daughter.
A Midsummer Night's Dream (William Dieterle and Max Reinhardt, 1935; Peter Hall, 1968; Michael Hoffman, 1999).
A Streetcar Named Desire (Elia Kazan, 1951). A film version of Tennessee Williams'

play that brought Marlon Brando to prominence – there is also a later made-for-television version.

A Taste of Honey (Tony Richardson, 1961). Film version of Shelagh Delaney's first and most famous play. A real slice of 'kitchen sink drama' with great performances and a period feel to it.

Agnes of God (Norman Jewison, 1985). Film version of this controversial play set in a convent. Agnes, a novice, is pregnant and she says her child is the son of God. Powerful performances.

As You Like It (Kenneth Branagh, 2006). Bryce Dallas Howard stars in Branagh's bold reworking of the play, setting it in nineteenth-century Japan. There are also two other versions readily available, one from 1936 with Laurence Olivier and the other from 1992 with James Fox.

Black Watch (John Tiffany, 2008). The filmed version of the National Theatre of Scotland's acclaimed production based on conversations with soldiers returning from Iraq. Beware: very strong language.

Coriolanus (BBC, 1984). Part of the BBC Shakespeare series, many other titles are also still available, with Alan Howard. Steven Berkoff's stage version is also available on DVD.

East (Steven Berkoff, 2000). Film of the stage production of Berkoff's play. This is Berkoff at his most expressive – and there are some stunning physical theatre set pieces. Beware: very strong language.

Hamlet (Laurence Olivier, 1948; Tony Richardson, 1969; Franco Zeffirelli, 1990; Kenneth Branagh, 1996).

King Lear (Peter Brook, 1971; Michael Elliott, 1983). The 2007 stage version with Ian McKellan is now available.

Macbeth (Orson Welles, 1948; Roman Polanski, 1971).

Othello (Wilson Milan, 2007). Eamonn Walker stars in this version filmed at the Globe Theatre. Other versions are available, including Ian McKellan as Iago from 1990.

Romeo and Juliet (Franco Zeffirelli, 1968; Baz Luhrmann, 1996).

Salome (Steven Berkoff, 1992). Berkoff's take on Oscar Wilde's play. A film of a stage production that contains all the Berkoff hallmarks but is here applied to Wilde's script.

The Caretaker (Clive Donner, 1963). Film version of Pinter's most famous play. Controversial at the time and still able to shock with its undercurrent of violence.

The Crucible (Nicholas Hytner, 1996). Film version of Arthur Miller's classic of witch-hunting in seventeenth-century Salem. Very faithful adaption of the original.

The Entertainer (Tony Richardson, 1960). Film version of John Osborne's play about the demise of a way of life for a variety performer. Great for the performance by Laurence Olivier in the role of Archie Rice.

The Glass Menagerie (Irving Rapper, 1950; Paul Newman, 1987). Film version of the Tennessee Williams play. Faithful to the original in content, if not always in style.

The Importance of Being Earnest (Anthony Asquith, 1952). Film version of Oscar Wilde's play. A bit old and creaky now but it represents really well the language and comedy of the situation which Wilde establishes. There is more than one version of the play on film, including a recent one with Rupert Everett (Oliver Parker, 2002).

The Laramie Project (Moses Kaufman, 2002). Film version of the docu-drama tracing the events leading up to the murder of Matthew Sheppard in Laramie, Wyoming, and the reactions of small-town America to this gay-hate crime.

The Trial (Steven Berkoff, 2002). Filmed stage version of Berkoff's adaptation of Kafka's novel. Has all the hallmarks of Berkoff's work.

Three Sisters (Laurence Olivier, 1970). A brooding and intense version of Chekhov's classic play, made for the American Film series and featuring Alan Bates and Joan Plowright.

Who's Afraid of Virginia Woolf (Mike Nichols, 1966). Film version of Albee's acerbic dissection of a couple at war. Great performances from Richard Burton and Elizabeth Taylor.

Glossary of useful words and phrases

The following glossary comprises drama and theatre words and phrases, most of which appear throughout this book. If you have reached this point, you are probably familiar with many of these words already. This list is to help you develop your own understanding of some of the more commonly used words and phrases you may come across on this course. The focus is mainly on those words and phrases associated with Unit 3 and Unit 4 but there are some more generic words included here too.

A glossary is not a dictionary or an encyclopaedia, so we do not, for example, include theatrical people or places here. You will have come across some useful information in the book and, if this has set you thinking about a particular person, play or place, then there are numerous websites that you could access in order to extend your knowledge – a list of some of these is included in Appendix 2. There is also a list of further reading and suggested viewing in Appendix 3. This is not an exhaustive list, but one which should prove accessible to you at this level of study, and one to which you and your teacher can add alternative texts and films that you may come across as part of the course.

The glossary signals for you where your thinking should lie in terms of being aware of the use of the language of drama and theatre at this level of study and, perhaps more importantly, how to spell it and what it means! We are aware of the demands of the quality of written communication with, in particular, Unit 4, and part of this is being able to use terms and expressions effectively.

Building a subject-specific vocabulary is something that will become very personal as your knowledge develops, and it is useful to be able to recognise drama and theatre terms as they occur, particularly if you are going on to study any aspect of drama or performance at higher education.

auditorium
Where the audience sits. In traditional theatres the audience and performers are separated by a curtain.

blocking
The process of arranging the actors within the space during rehearsal so that the action, events and key relationships are visible to the audience in the performance.

box set
A set that as far as possible represents the space in which the action takes place, usually referring to a room in a house, and so-called as it creates a 'box' into which the actors enter and exit through realistic doors and are confined in the space, usually not breaking the fourth wall.

chronological
Something that is presented in order of the events as they occur in time.

concept
An idea that responds to the original and brings it to life to incorporate an understanding of text in relation to shaping audience response using elements of theatre.

conventions of the theatre
Accepted performance techniques and ideas that might be employed in order to shape audience response.

designer
Responsible for creating the look and feel of the production. There are usually a number of contributors to design in the professional theatre, each responsible for a particular aspect of design, including set, lighting and costume.

devising
Creating performance from a given stimulus, usually a collaborative process for actors.

director
The person in control of all aspects of the production, primarily in relation to the actors but also responsible for the ideas to inspire the design considerations to support the overall vision. Most directors will work collaboratively but will exercise the right to have the final say.

elements of theatre
The parts that make up the whole of the experience that could include, for example, acting techniques, design skills and director's interpretation.

Elizabethan theatre
From the time period of Queen Elizabeth I – usually associated with Shakespeare and Marlowe, but other influential playwrights were also at work during this period.

ensemble
Usually refers to the collective of the company where there is equality within the performance and often opportunities for multi-roling contributions to the piece.

epic theatre
A term coined by Brecht in which major world events are seen through the eyes of individuals.

episodic
A play written in short scenes or episodes that help create an almost cinematic feel for the performance and encourages a fast-paced production.

flats
Traditionally canvas screens stretched on to wooden frames, fitted together to create box sets, for example, and to give an illusion of something more solid. Also used more symbolically to create and define spaces during performances, and may be free-standing or flown in and out of spaces.

flies
The area above the stage, usually hidden from view from which flats, screens or lights can be flown in and out of the stage space below. A very complex system of ropes and pulleys was originally used to fly scenery in and out of spaces, operated by trained stage-hands.

fourth wall
The imaginary wall that separates actor and audience in what may be seen as a traditional proscenium arch theatre, usually with a box set that often represents a room, the 'fourth wall' of which is the one that faces the audience.

genre
The style in which the play is written.

improvising
Exploring character and situation to gain a greater understanding of the who, why and where of the relationships. Sometimes leads to performance but is often used as a means of supporting more developed work around scripts.

interpretation
The approach to a text which a director will adopt to create a version of the play in performance that has a particular stamp on it. Look at the work of Katie Mitchell, for example.

lighting desk
The board or screen from which the lighting for the performance is operated once rigged, set and programmed.

model
Many designers will create a scale model of the set so that the actors and director can see how it might look in its final form. These are increasingly being created and imagined using 3D technology rather than real models.

non-linear
A play that has a structure that moves backwards and forwards in time in relation to the events unfolding for the audience. It may start with the final scene and then go back to the beginning to show how the events unfolded to create this moment.

Old Comedy
A distinct period in theatrical development in Greek theatre. Usually refers to work that is anti-democratic or seen to be sceptical towards all forms of authority – the work of Aristophanes, for example.

physical theatre
A term from the late twentieth century to mean an approach to performance that uses highly developed physical skills to represent character and situation, with actors often representing location as well as characters in the performance.

plotting session
A session that looks at the technical elements of the production, not including actors, at which the state of light and sound for the performance is set.

practitioner
An individual or company with influence that stretches into other companies and the work of other individuals, and shapes the work of these others in response to the original ideas.

proscenium
The traditional picture frame type of stage, usually – but not always – with a curtain. The audience looks through the arch to the actors who are separated from the audience by the frame. This type of staging is usually, but not always, associated with the box set.

proscenium arch
The actual opening of the frame itself.

read-through
The time early on in rehearsals where the actors gather with the director and read through the script with assigned roles.

rig
The process by which a flying scenic element or light is put up. Also refers to the physical structure (for example, lighting rig).

sightline
Vital during rehearsals. The director needs to ensure that action is visible to the audience within the performance space. Some theatres offer seats for sale with 'limited visibility', which usually has nothing to do with sightlines but often means that the building itself has areas that have obstructions in place – pillars holding up the gallery, for example. There is not really a great deal a director can do about this.

stage weights
Heavy metal blocks that are used to support the legs of free-standing screens or flats and are useful in adding weight to scenic elements that need to stay put during the performance.

tech.
Abbreviation for the technical rehearsal for the production, often put with the dress rehearsal to create 'dress and tech'.

tempo
The overall speed at which a character thinks and does things.

Theatre of Cruelty
The theatre of Antonin Artaud. A forerunner of 'In-yer-face Theatre' that challenges the audience on every level and sets out to make them think about the human condition. Artaud's use of the word 'cruelty' needs further exploration, as it encompasses a range of ideas for performers and designers as well as the audience.

thrust stage
A stage that comes out into the audience that creates a platform for the actors very close to the audience. Traditionally this is associated with the Globe Theatre.

total theatre
Associated with physical theatre and arising from the work of, among others, Steven Berkoff. Total theatre immerses the actor completely in the exploration of physical representation of character and situation.

tragedy
A style of theatre stemming from Ancient Greece and developed through the centuries by playwrights, most famously Shakespeare, in which the protagonist or hero suffers serious misfortune, usually as a result of human and divine actions.

Index

A2 year: advantages 4; challenges of 160; deadlines, importance of 6; diaries 11; grading 7; skills and knowledge expected 3–4, 5, 6; working together *see* working together; and written work 22

The Accrington Pals (Whelan) 30, 35

Acropolis 77

Aeschylus 76

A Funny Thing Happened on the Way to the Forum (Sondheim) 76

Alexander the Great 77

An Actor's Guide to Getting Work (Dunmore) 164

analysis 11

annotation 128–30; concept or interpretation 130; drawing/sketch of proposed staging 128–29; focusing of thoughts 71; historical context 130; index, including 129; rehearsal techniques and methods 129

Anthem for Doomed Youth (Owen), as stimulus material 32, 35

Aristophanes 75–78; *see also Lysistrata* (Aristophanes)

Aristotle 75

Artaud, Antonin 177

assessment: development and structure (Unit 3) 23, 44–46; research and exploration (Unit 3) 36–37; section A 95–98; section B 109–10; Unit 3 23–24; Unit 4 12, 63–64

AS year: drama words and phrases 12; making connections 90; rehearsal strategies 86; skills developed in 4; theatre evaluation 139; and Unit 3 performance 47

Athens/Athenian theatre 76, 77

audience response, controlling 44

auditorium 173

Augier, Émile 80

Barrie, J. M. 81

Benavente, José 81

Berkoff, Steven 137, 177

Birmingham Six 42

blocking 174

Bogdanov, Michael 148–50

Bonds of Interest (Benavente) 81

boxes, theatre 81–82

box set 83, 174

Buchner, Georg *see Woyzeck* (Buchner)

Caesar, Julius 76

call-up papers/travel documents, as stimulus material 33, 35

career choices for Drama and Theatre Studies students 22

Cartwright, Jim 10–11

Chekhov, Anton 132

The Cherry Orchard (Chekhov) 132

Chorus 76

chronological order 174

class segregation, in theatres 82

'closet' drama 80

comedies 75

Comedy of Errors 76

computers: Internet as source on theatre productions 137; websites 21, 95, 164, 165–68; word-count facilities on 19

concept/interpretation: annotation 130; definition of concept 174; section B 103–4, 111; *see also* interpretation
The Conference of Drama Schools 164
connections, making: historical, in Unit 4 146–51; in section A 87; in section B 104–8
conventions, theatre 174
coursework, Unit 3 9
Cradle Song (G M Sierra) 81
Cratinus 76
criminal justice system 41
The Crucible (Miller) 39, 40, 43
Cyrano de Bergerac (Rostand) 80

Darvell brothers 42
deadlines, meeting 6, 18
deconstruction of examination questions 158–59
deconstruction of script 24
Dee, John 79
designers 174
development and structure (Unit 3) 38–46; assessment of 23, 44–46; language use 46; routes 1–5 40–41; script, developing 39–42; from stimulus materials 43–44; tragedy 41–42; worked examples 44–45
devised work 25, 174
diaries 10–11
Dionysus, Theatre of 77
directors, role of: accessing the examination questions 126–27, 161; craft of director 121; function of director 121–23, 174; 'given and structured' purpose, section A 92–93; and the interpretation 126; in rehearsals 123–24; in section A (Unit 4) 85; in section A or B (Unit 4) 120–27; and Unit 4 decisions 66
Doctor Faustus (Marlowe): context 78–80; plot 117; as possible set text for Unit 4 16; staging interpretation of 130
drama: language of 11–13, 46; theatre distinguished 3
drama degree 163
Drama School 8, 163–64
Dumas, Alexander 80
Dunmore, Simon 164
duologues 47

Echegaray, José 81
Edexcel: Drama and Theatre Studies Specification 3, 22; website 21, 95
elements of theatre 174
Elizabethan theatre 16, 78, 174; and Unit 4 decisions 118
ensemble 175
epic theatre 175
episodic plays 175
Euripides 76
evaluation 52–57; meaning 11, 52–53; theatre *see* theatre evaluation; worked examples 53–57
examination advice, Unit 4: accessing the questions 126–27, 161; deconstruction of questions 158–59; focusing thoughts 71–72; gathering of thoughts 68–69; opening paragraphs 73; ordering thoughts 70; quality of written communication 67–68; research notes 155; starters and closers 72–73; worked examples 73–74; writing things down 69
Examination Board: deadlines set by 6; Examiners appointed by 20; Moderators appointed by 21; and section A (Unit 4) 64; on word limits 18
examiners: relationship with 142–45; role 20, 21; Unit 4, assessing 63
expressionism 80
extension activities: craft of director 121; directors, role of 85; historical perspective, exploring 148–49; important plays/playwrights, time periods 119; Internet use 138; language of drama 13, 46; notice-board, creating 34; planning rehearsals 94; practitioners 106; purpose of rehearsal 125; rehearsal techniques 124; stimulus, responding to 9; theatrical timeline 15; Unit 3 26; Unit 4 67; word counts 37; working on text responses 97; and YG&T 7
extension material, and homework activities 7–8

Fiennes, Ralph 135
flats (canvas screens) 175
flies (area above stage) 175
fourth wall 175
framing for murder 41–42
French theatre 80

Galsworthy, John 81
genre 175
Globe Theatre, London 14, 79
glossaries 68–69, 71
grades 7
Greek drama/Ancient Greece: comedies 75, 76; knowledge of 13; stages and presentation styles 77–78; theatrical timeline 16; tragedies 75, 177; and Unit 4 decisions 118; *see also* Athens/Athenian theatre
Gregory, Lady Augusta 81
group sizes 24
Guildford Four 42

Hauptmann, G. 80
Higgins, Claire 75
historical periods 146–51; from 525 BC-AD 65, 119, 146, 152; from 1564–1720 119, 147, 152; from 1828–1914 119, 147, 152; exploring historical perspective 148–51; extension activity 148–49; focus of historical perspective 134; Unit 4, making connections in 146–51
Hope Theatre, London 79
Hugo, Victor 80

improvisation 175
index, including in annotation 129
Industrial Revolution 81
interpretation: definition 175; and directors 126; general points 112; of script 24; in section B 101–2; *see also* concept/interpretation

Jones, Henry Arthur 80

Kemble, Charles 83
key words 98–99, 159
King John 83
King Lear 49–51
knowledge of Drama and Theatre Studies, increasing 13

language, of drama 11–13, 46
Law, Jude 135
library, school or college 28
lighting desk 175
lists, usefulness of 71
literary drama 80
Little Theatre movement 80
live theatre, evaluation (section C) 152–55
Lumley, Joanna 132
Lysistrata (Aristophanes): as anti-war play 147; context 75–78; plot 117; as possible set text for Unit 4 16; presentation stages/styles 77–78; staging interpretation of 130

Macbeth 24
mark allocation: Supporting Written Evidence Document (SWED) 58; Unit 3 23, 27, 31, 38, 52; Unit 4 64, 65, 99, 109
Marlowe, C. 78–80; *see also Doctor Faustus* (Marlowe)
McCarthy, John 40
McCarthyism 43
McKellan, Ian 135
medals, as stimulus materials 31, 34
melodrama 82
Menander 76–77
A Midsummer Night's Dream (worked example) 144
Miller, Arthur 39, 40, 43
miscarriages of justice 41–42
model of set 176
moderators, role 21
monologues 47
morality plays 16
murder, framing for 41–42
music-halls 81, 82
mystery plays 16

Napper, Robert 41
National Theatre 135
National Youth Theatre 164
naturalism 80
New Comedy 76–77
Nickell, Rachel 41–42
nineteenth-century theatre 16, 118

non-linear plays 176
notebooks: gathering of thoughts in 68; as working diaries 10–11
note taking: colour coding 141; contents covered 156–57; drama research 29; highlighting of notes 68; section C 139–42
notice-board, creating 33, 34

Old Comedy 75, 76, 176
opening paragraphs 73
orchestra, Greek theatre 77
Owen, W. 32, 35

parodoi (paths) 78
Passion Flower (Benavente) 81
performance: live, preparing for 136–39; Unit 2 47–48; Unit 3 47–51
Phipps, C. J. 82
Phlyates 76
physical theatre 176
Pinero, Sir Arthur Wing 80
Plautus (Roman playwright) 76
playhouses, open-air 79
playwright's original intentions, interpreting 103–4
plotting sessions 176
The Poetics (Aristotle) 75
poppies, as stimulus materials 32, 34–35
practical exercises 8, 51, 91–95
practitioners 72, 105, 176; extension activities 106
preparation: role of teacher in preparation process 135–36; worked example 113
Principal Examiner 20
proscenium 176
proscenium arch 176
psychological profiling 42
public houses 81

QWC (quality of written communication) 60

Raleigh, Sir Walter 79
read-through 176
Realism movement 83
rehearsals: directors in 123–24; functions 125; planning 94; possible approaches to texts in 90–91; purpose 91, 124–25; strategies 86–89
rehearsal techniques 85–86, 87; annotation 129; extension activity 124
research and exploration (Unit 3) 27–37; assessment of 23, 36–37; definition of research 28; researching with focus 88–89; research notes 154–57; routes 30; text 35–36; word counts 37; worked example 36–37
research notes 154–55; compiling 155–57
resources centres 28
Rig 176
Road (Cartwright) 10–11
Robinson, J. T. 82
Romeo and Juliet 148–50
Rose Theatre, London 79
Rostand, Edmond 80
round theatres 138
The Royal Exchange Theatre, Manchester 138
Royal Shakespeare Company 135, 137

SAMs (Sample Assessment Material) 93, 95, 98
Sardou, Victorien 80
Scholey, Annabel 132
School of Night 79
Scribe, Eugène 80
script-based work 24, 39–42; and devised drama 25
section A: assessment 95–98; connections, making 87; key words 98–99; possible approaches to texts in rehearsal 90–91; practical drama activities 91–95; rehearsal strategies 86–89
section A (Unit 4): approaches to texts in rehearsal 90–91; directors, role of 85; focus of 84–85; general approach to 84; length of extracts in 92; making choices 118–19; mark allocation 64; practical exercises 91–95; preparation, worked example 113; rehearsal strategies 86–89; rehearsal techniques 85–86, 87; researching with focus 88–89;

texts for 65, 116–19; worked examples 93, 96–97
section B (Unit 4): assessment 109–10; concept or interpretation 103–4, 111; connections, making 104–8; focusing of thoughts 71; general approach to 100–103; general points, interpretations 112; getting started 112–14; interpretations, exploring 111–15; making choices 118–19; mark allocation 64; preparation, worked example 113; texts for 65, 116–19; updating decisions 114–15; worked examples 107–8, 113, 114
section C (Unit 4) 131–45; evaluating live theatre 152–55; examiner, relationship with 142–45; live performance, preparing for 136–39, 147–48; mark allocation 64; note taking 139–42; role of teacher in preparation process 135–36; staging conditions, strategies 136; worked examples 140, 144
sentences, and glossaries 68, 69, 71
Shakespeare, William: *Comedy of Errors* 76; and Elizabethan theatre 78; and Globe Theatre 79; *King John* 83; *King Lear* 49–51; *Macbeth* 24; *A Midsummer Night's Dream* 144; *Romeo and Juliet* 148–50
Shaw, George Bernard 81
Shoreditch, London (first theatre at) 79
Sierra, Gregorio Martìnez 81
sightline 177
skene (scene building) 78
Sondheim, Stephen 76
Sophocles 76, 77
Spartans 77
spelling 12
stage weights 177
Stagg, Colin 41–42, 43
staging conditions, strategies 136
Stewart, Patrick 135
stimulus materials, responding to: development and structure 38, 43–44; extension activity 9; researching/exploring 27–28, 31–35; script-based work 24
Sudermann, H. 80
Supporting Written Evidence Document (SWED) 58–61; deadlines 6; development and structure (Unit 3) 45–46; evaluation evidence recorded in 53; questions addressed in 58; research and exploration (Unit 3) 36–37; routes 1–5 59–60; starting point for 29; word limits 9; writing as individual while working on group project 60–61
SWED *see* Supporting Written Evidence Document (SWED)

teacher-assessor: role in preparation process 135–36; and role of Moderator 21; Unit 3 assessment 63
tech. 177
tempo 177
Tennant, David 135
Terence (Roman playwright) 76
texts for Unit 4, context 74–83; *Doctor Faustus* (Marlowe) 78–80; *Lysistrata* (Aristophanes) 75–78; *Woyzeck* (Buchner) 80–83
theatre: drama distinguished 3; evaluation of *see* theatre evaluation
theatre evaluation 152–57; focusing of thoughts 71; live theatre (section C) 152–55; research notes 154–57
Theatre of Cruelty 177
Theatre of Dionysus 77
Theatres Act (1843) 81
theatrical timeline 13, 15–17
theatron (watching place) 77
Thespis 77
thoughts: focusing of 71–72; gathering of 68–69; ordering of 70
thrust stage 177
total theatre 177
touring companies 135–36
tragedy 41–42, 75, 177
twentieth-century theatre 16–17
twenty-first century theatre (modern times) 17, 147

UCAS application 7, 164
Unit 1 90, 155–56
Unit 2 47–48, 90
Unit 3: allocation of teaching time 23;

assessment objectives 23–24; coursework 9; deadlines 6, 18; devised work 25; evaluating performance of a piece 55–57; evaluating process of a piece 53–55; general approach to 161; group sizes 24; mark allocation 23, 27, 31, 38, 52; objectives 160; routes 26; script and devised drama 25; script-based work 24; word limits 18
Unit 4: assessment objectives 12, 63–64; decisions required for 66–67; examination advice 67–74; examiner, assessed by 63; focus of 65; historical connections 146–51; importance of 65; mark allocation 64, 65, 99, 109; objectives 160; overview of texts 64; skills and knowledge expected 66–67; three texts, context 74–83; time periods 15

Wanamaker, Sam 79
websites 21, 95, 164, 165–68
Whelan, Peter 30, 35
Wilde, Oscar 80
Witches of Warboys story 43, 44–45
word counts 19, 37
word limits 9, 18, 139
working together 4–5, 33, 34; group projects 60–61; section A (Unit 4) 94–95
workshop activities 91–94
The World and His Wife (Echegaray) 81
Woyzeck (Buchner): context 80–83; plot 118; as possible set text for Unit 4, 16; as worked example 73–74, 96–97
written communication 8–11
Written Examination, date for 6
wrongful accusation 41–42

Yeats, W. B. 81
Young Gifted and Talented Programme (YG&T) 7